Reimagining
Anti-Oppression
Social Work Research

D1571643

Reimagining
Anti-Oppression
Social Work Research

Edited by
Henry Parada and Samantha Wehbi

CANADIAN
SCHOLARS

Toronto | Vancouver

Reimagining Anti-Oppression Social Work Research
Edited by Henry Parada and Samantha Wehbi

First published in 2017 by
Canadian Scholars
425 Adelaide Street West, Suite 200
Toronto, Ontario
M5V 3C1

www.canadianscholars.ca

Library and Archives Canada Cataloguing in Publication

Reimagining anti-oppression social work research / edited by Henry Parada and Samantha Wehbi.

Includes bibliographical references and index.

Issued in print and electronic formats.
ISBN 978-1-55130-976-7 (softcover).--ISBN 978-1-55130-977-4 (PDF).--ISBN 978-1-55130-978-1 (EPUB)

1. Social work with minorities--Research--Canada. I. Wehbi, Samantha, 1969-, editor II. Parada, Henry, 1959-, editor

HV3176.R457 2017   362.840072'071   C2017-902772-7   C2017-902773-5

Text design by Brad Horning
Cover design by Em Dash Design
Cover photo © Samantha Wehbi, from the *Pieces of Place* series

17   18   19   20   21   5   4   3   2   1

Canada

Contents

Section III: Valuing Fluidity and Unknowing

Preface:
Anti-Oppression Research
Epistemologies, Principles, Directions

Henry Parada, Associate Professor,
School of Social Work, Ryerson University

Samantha Wehbi, Professor,
School of Social Work, Ryerson University

Research for social change has always found a willing ally in anti-oppression epistemology and principles. This book focuses on examples of research guided by anti-oppression to elucidate what research for social change might look like. We suggest that anti-oppression is not a specific and fixed methodology but a theoretical and epistemological guide to how and why research takes place, while also not claiming that all methodologies are compatible with anti-oppressive knowledge and values. Rogers (2012) argues that anti-oppressive research offers a way to introduce a discussion of power into the research process, which departs from dominant research methodologies where researchers conduct "research on 'subjects' who may have little involvement in the research" (p. 867). Indeed, Indigenous scholars have long argued for the need to decentre Eurocentric knowledge and worldviews, noting how the process of research has reflected and reinforced the process of exploitation and marginalization and inviting us to critically examine our involvement in research (Baskin, 2011; Hart, 2009; Kovach, 2005; Lavallée, 2009). Instead, anti-oppressive approaches to research revalue the role of participants and in fact begin with challenging and troubling "the connections between how knowledge is created, what knowledge is produced, and who is entitled to engage in these processes" (Brown & Strega, 2005, p. 7).

As such, knowledge creation and communication processes are at the heart of anti-oppressive approaches to practice, as much as the substantive topics dealt with in research and in this book. Keeping in mind this understanding of anti-oppression as an epistemological base for research, the emphasis of the book is not on critiquing dominant modes of research, as the methodological scholarship is replete with such examinations. Put another way, this book is not yet another text offering critiques of top-down, researcher-imposed, community-absent research agendas, but instead focuses on the alternatives offered through anti-oppressive research. Our exploration is guided by the following central questions: How can anti-oppression research contribute to a social change goal, and what are some of the underlying values, desired outcomes, and methodologies guiding anti-oppressive research? As such, the chapters present insights into how various methodologies such as phenomenology, arts-based inquiry, critical discourse analysis, autoethnography, and others may be undertaken in conversation and in negotiation with anti-oppression principles.

Hence, far from being a purely descriptive endeavour, the chapters in this book attempt to chart the tensions that emerge when anti-oppression principles enter into dialogue with research methodologies. The chapter by Preston and Redgrift outlines these principles while specifically examining how they may or may not be compatible with a phenomenological approach. This discussion is further complicated by the work of George as well as that of Wehbi, who both explore the use of creative arts such as photography and performance in implementing research based on anti-oppression and anti-colonialism principles and in communicating its findings. The authors all contend that treading consciously and critically in the terrain of anti-oppression principles as they co-exist with research methodologies can assist us in moving beyond the familiar and traditional uses of research, advancing it instead as a way of furthering social transformation.

These tensions are further illustrated through chapters that provide examples of research projects that take up the question of what anti-oppression–informed methodologies might look like on the ground. The emphasis here is on how these methodologies are implemented with specific examples of working with historically marginalized and activist communities. The focus of these chapters is not on the "vulnerabilities" of such populations but on strategies of resistance and how these could be furthered using anti-oppression principles. For example, Pyne and colleagues explore the uses of anti-oppressive research principles in combating transphobia in Chapter 1. Similarly, in Chapter 2, El-Lahib explores the intersections between anti-oppression and anti-colonialism to further disability rights. In their chapters, Moffatt and colleagues, Yee, and Smith all examine how anti-oppression principles, along with anti-racism and whiteness lenses, can elucidate the experiences of workers in social service organizations.

In keeping with the anti-oppressive foundations of this book, the discussion would not be complete without turning these lenses on the researcher's own subjectivities and processes of working. Focusing on autoethnography and using anti-racism and decolonizing lenses, Friedman and Silver each examine their own experiences as researchers and educators engaged in anti-oppression work. Friedman helps us to deconstruct modernist notions of identity that underlie much of research, while Silver challenges us to examine what we can learn from Indigenous worldviews and research principles.

THEMES AND DIRECTIONS

The chapters in this book are divided into three sections, each addressing a major theme in order to answer our guiding questions about anti-oppressive research. The first theme explores the importance of community involvement in research in ways that challenge our understandings of engagement, control, and the researcher's role in the process of knowledge production. The second theme moves from considering processes of community engagement to examining how anti-oppressive research can unfold in organizational settings, pointing to inherent challenges and tensions. The final theme calls for a revaluing of fluidity and uncertainty, moving away from overly modernist ways of conceptualizing identity, research, and knowledge production.

Conversations and Negotiations: Engaging with Community

The first section examines how anti-oppression can and needs to engage with different methodologies, while focusing on the processes of engagement with community. The emphasis here is on the social responsibility of the researcher toward social groups at the heart of our concern as anti-oppressive practitioners and researchers. Considering the importance of the process of knowledge creation, the authors emphasize the need to bring to the forefront the voices of marginalized communities by questioning who has the epistemic and ethical authority and privilege to speak on behalf of marginalized communities. In a now-classic text on speaking for the "other," Alcoff (1991/1992) examines who has the authority and privilege to speak on behalf of the other and to represent experiences of marginalization. The author notes that, even in situations where researchers and practitioners are seeking to challenge oppressive social conditions, there is a potential to replicate experiences of marginalization by privileging dominant representations and voices. Through examples from grassroots research projects, the authors in this volume argue for the importance of challenging the role of the expert researcher and ensuring that anti-oppressive research privileges the experiences and voices of people at the margins, not only as recipients of services, but also as activists in their own lives and realities.

In Chapter 1, Pyne and colleagues explore how research process and outcomes have been reclaimed by trans communities in reframing their own experiences. This chapter examines choice of methodologies and argues that while quantitative methodologies are rooted in Eurocentric underpinnings, they do hold potential for use in anti-oppressive research. Through an examination of Trans PULSE, a community-based and controlled, health-focused research project, the authors illustrate their contention that the "quantification of lived experience" can be a site of marginalization, but can also be a way of resisting oppression depending on the context of use. The authors discuss key methodological debates in research seeking social justice, specifically the differences between community participation and control of the data and outcomes of research, as well as knowledge production in terms of issues of research ownership and representation of marginalized communities.

Similarly, Chapter 2 offers key concepts and principles that can guide anti-oppressive research in ways that favour community control. El-Lahib focuses on anti-oppressive research as it intersects with critical disability studies. Specifically, the author highlights key principles related to the importance of context, the role of the researcher and researched community, the research process, and research outcomes, illustrating these through examples from disability rights and justice organizing in the global South. This chapter is infused with an analysis of North/South power relations, guided by ideas from postcolonial disability scholarship to examine issues related to representation, positionality of the researcher, and relationships with community, as well as the importance of understanding the broader socio-political and historical contexts within which research projects are undertaken.

Picking up the theme of how anti-oppression needs to engage with various methodologies while maintaining an emphasis on community control, issues of representation, and voice, George offers alternatives to privileged representations with a study that illustrates how communities can tell their own stories through the use of creative forms. While Pyne et al. and El-Lahib focus on the processes of research, in Chapter 3, George attends to the communication of findings and proposes critical arts-based research mobilization (CABRM) as a way to deal with concerns about being able to present multiple and differing perspectives. Presenting this complexity is in keeping with the anti-oppressive principles of valuing the voices of participants in the research process and outcomes. The chapter focuses on the use of performance poetry as an example of CABRM to bring to the fore multiple and differing voices, specifically as this relates to knowledge production and the outcomes of research contributing to social justice and change. In order to illustrate these ideas, the author provides the example of the successes and challenges of a study on issues experienced by racialized older immigrants, which highlighted issues of voice, authority, and participation in the research process.

Adding to the discussion about using art-infused methodologies to privilege multiple voices and how we represent our work with the marginalized other, Wehbi proposes, in Chapter 4, the need to look critically at issues of representation in visual forms. Issues of voice and representation arise as visual images can and have been used to support colonial discourses historically, and to reinforce neocolonial readings of North/South relations as they connect specifically to international development and practices with community. The author suggests that how we construct the other is as much about written text as it is about visual representations, and she argues for the need for greater engagement with visual data in social work research. Specifically, Wehbi explores the link between photography and anti-oppressive research and contends that there is a need to move beyond our current focus on photovoice, which at times can lead to further marginalization of participants, to the adoption of critical visual research principles that are in line with those of anti-oppression. The chapter provides a discussion of how the analysis of visual data can be undertaken and what needs to guide such a process of understanding image narratives, including a clearly articulated theoretical framework and an understanding of the diverse elements of an image, as well as a reading of broader socio-political contextual factors such as histories of colonialism. To illustrate these points, the author explores international development images of community practice through a postcolonial lens, and engages in a semiotic analysis of a recurring image that highlights whiteness and the reproduction of neocolonial discourses.

For social work, this engagement with art in practice and in research holds the promise of challenging not only *what* we know, by enriching the scope of experiences that we can access, but also *how* we know, by challenging positivist and rationalist modes of knowledge production. Social work authors such as Chambon (2008); Hafford-Letchfield, Leonard, and Couchman (2012); Huss (2009); and Walton (2012) argue for the need to move social work beyond its focus on solely text and to engage with modes of knowledge production that revalue expressive and iterative ways of accessing experience and knowledge. By doing so, we contribute to creating alternative discourses with and about clients, communities, and social work practices that address not only textual but also visual representations.

Unfolding Anti-Oppressive Research in Organizational Settings

Shifting the discussion from looking at anti-oppressive research practice and principles in communities, the second theme in this book is the need to examine what happens when we examine anti-oppression in organizations. The authors in this section provide examples of research guided by anti-oppression principles and the challenges, tensions, and possibilities that arise in working within social service organizations.

In Chapter 5, Moffatt and colleagues illustrate ideas about anti-oppressive research in organizations through a case study of anti-oppression and anti-racism change in a feminist organization. Through this study, the authors present organizational struggles through the narratives of workers discussing the tensions and challenges involved in resisting whiteness and embracing anti-racism lenses and orientations, alongside anti-oppression principles at the level of programming, personal interactions, and professionalization. Key issues addressed include issues of participation and representation, as well as identity politics, and how these intersect and interlock with various forms of oppression.

In Chapter 6, Yee explores how and why it is important to conduct research examining processes of whiteness, white supremacy, and racialization, and how these unfold and are reinforced in organizational structures, practices, and processes. The author contends that it is important to uncover the often hidden processes of whiteness and white supremacy that operate in the social service organizations where we practice. This contention is illustrated with the proposition of a methodological approach and principles to challenge white supremacy in social service agencies, such as scrutinizing dominant hidden assumptions; focusing not only on outcomes of research but on processes; and examining institutional and organizational arrangements and practices. In doing so, the author engages with ideas from the scholarship on critical race theories, including discussions of white supremacy, racialization, racism, and colonialism.

Finally, in Chapter 7, Smith describes a research design used to explore how activist social workers navigate workplace contexts during times of neoliberal restructuring. Specifically, the author focuses on what happens to anti-oppression aspirations and practices within such changing contexts. The author explores this topic through a biographical research study with social workers who have extensive experience in child welfare or primary health care, examining how their identities and subjectivities are simultaneously at play with their workplace performances. A key discussion that emerges through this research and these narratives is the importance of recognizing the role of resistance and shifting subjectivities, which we discuss in the final section of the book.

Valuing Fluidity and Uncertainty

A final theme that emerges from the ideas presented in this book relates to the need to challenge static conceptions of identity in research. The authors in this section urge us to re-evaluate the importance of fluidity and uncertainty in how we think about research, communities, marginalized groups, activism, and knowledge production. A common thread tying the chapters together is the need for reflexive engagement with the research process. For the authors in this section, engaging in anti-oppressive research reflexively implies standing firmly in a state of discomfort in order to deal with our epistemological ignorance, refusal, and privilege. As such, reflexivity is not an end goal, but a means to an end exercised by taking responsibility for how we contribute to knowledge through, and beyond, dominance.

Chapter 8 by Preston and Redgrift explores the links between anti-oppression research principles and phenomenology, and emphasizes the importance of reflexive approaches to research, as well as the need to question essentializing notions of lived experience and identity. The authors contend that phenomenological research is a form of anti-oppressive research, even though there may be tensions between these approaches. Through this discussion, the authors explore the potential alignment of phenomenology with anti-oppression in terms of issues such as the positioning of the researcher with regards to their study; the role of power in the research relationship between researcher and participants; the role of the researcher and participants in terms of knowledge production and how this relates to data collection, interpretation, and research outcomes; and differences in understanding the essence of lived experiences. The authors conclude the chapter with a discussion of potential ways to address the tensions between phenomenology and anti-oppressive approaches to research and highlight the role of reflexivity in mitigating some of these tensions.

For Friedman, reflexivity is also a process of taking responsibility to challenge hegemonic ways of knowing. By turning the focus on herself as a researcher, practitioner, and educator, the author questions racial binaries that prevent us from understanding the world beyond the identity markers prescribed through the operation of whiteness. Chapter 9 explores the margins of identity and the shifting terrain of identity markers through an autoethnographical account of Friedman's own diasporic identity, in terms of ethnicity and race specifically related to her own Jewish-Arab background. Her discussion aims to expand an understanding of anti-oppression by challenging the fixity of identity markers. Friedman's account takes the reader through a methodological discussion of autoethnography, followed by an examination of decolonization, race, and ethnicity as they intersect and interlock to form and disrupt notions of identity.

In the case of Chapter 10 by Silver, the classroom as a site of struggle and potential resistance is explored through the author's own engagement in reflexivity. In this final chapter, Silver shares an autoethnographic account of her own experiences as an educator in an anti-oppressive program. By sharing her journey of challenging herself to examine her own teaching practice, she illustrates how we can unwittingly reproduce Eurocentrism even as we seek to resist it through anti-oppressive education. In this critical story, the author examines how she contributed to epistemic violence in the classroom around Indigenous issues. She critically examines her role in perpetuating and reproducing colonialism in how she taught about research methodologies, even as her aim was to expose students to anti-oppressive research. The chapter engages with the key concepts of reflexivity, decolonization, and the need to embrace a position of unknowing.

We end this preface with an invitation to engage with us in the issues outlined in the pages of this book. A key challenge is to find a way to contribute to social transformation while maintaining critical understanding and reflexivity on our role as anti-oppressive researchers. In doing so, we engage in reshaping not only *what* we know but also *how* we know, in the hope of moving social work research closer to epistemologies that challenge dominance in all its forms.

Section I

Conversations and Negotiations
Processes of Engaging with Community

1

Taking the Pulse, Making Trans People Count

Quantitative Method as Social Justice Strategy in the Trans PULSE Project

Jake Pyne, Trudeau and Vanier Scholar, Doctoral Student, School of Social Work, McMaster University

Greta Bauer, Associate Professor and Graduate Chair, Epidemiology and Biostatistics, Schulich School of Medicine and Dentistry, Western University

Rebecca Hammond, Nurse and Community-Based Researcher

Robb Travers, Associate Professor and Chair, Department of Health Sciences, Wilfrid Laurier University

As anti-oppressive researchers increasingly seek to articulate the principles guiding their work, methodological choices are a topic of debate. With an undeniably Eurocentric underpinning, quantitative social and health sciences methods have been critiqued both on epistemological and political grounds. For some, these methods are incompatible with a social justice or feminist agenda (Graham, 1983), and have come to represent, as Strega (2005) suggests, "the master's tools" (p. 200). As a team of social justice–oriented researchers working on a project that includes quantitative methods, we wonder if this tells the whole story.

In this chapter, we present a case study of Trans PULSE, a "community controlled" research project exploring the impact of social exclusion on the health of transgender (trans) people in Ontario, Canada. Against a backdrop in which the ongoing psychiatric control of trans lives is justified vis-à-vis "scientific" authority, our team of trans community members, service providers, and academic researchers sought to influence health and social policy with evidence produced through a quantitative survey methodology. While Trans PULSE utilized a multi-method program of research, we focus here on the quantitative phase of our project because (a) it was the more substantial phase of the study, and (b) we feel the field of anti-oppressive research could benefit from more in-depth discussion of quantitative design. Though we observe the importance of the many critiques of positivist methodologies, we propose a fuller discussion of research strategy in context. Highlighting a case that called for engagement with, rather than disengagement from, mainstream research methods, we caution against abandoning the field of traditional research to those who may lack social justice goals. While the quantification of lived experience can be complicit with marginalization, we argue it may also be resistant to some of the forms that marginalization takes. We propose that methodologies ought to be considered, lauded, rejected, or adapted as the case may be, within the context of their use, and we suggest that we remain attentive to all sites where critical action might take place.

METHODOLOGICAL DEBATES IN SOCIAL JUSTICE RESEARCH

Denzin and Lincoln (2005) note that, since the 1960s, researchers have drawn "battle lines" between quantitative and qualitative research traditions. Devotion to one of these two designs has been compared to the religious worship of different gods (Beck, 2006) or to conflicts between cultures (Mahoney & Goertz, 2006). Rooted in positivist science, quantitative research is said to employ deductive theory testing to measure and explain phenomena and produce findings with statistical significance (Bryman, 2008). Qualitative research, on the other hand, is said to occur in the natural world, analyzing lived experience to inductively generate theory and rich description (Bryman, 2008). Yet methodological debates are about more than the absence or presence of measurement. Political rather than technical in focus, these debates generate potent epistemological questions regarding what constitutes knowledge, how we know what we know, and who can be said to produce knowledge.

For researchers concerned with social justice, there are many vantage points from which to critique quantitative methods. Researchers working from an interpretivist stance have charged that the positivist claim to objectivity occludes the ideological investment of the researcher and fails to reveal the worldview of participants (Denzin & Lincoln, 2005). Critical theorists of many kinds, including feminists, critical race theorists, Indigenous scholars, and queer theorists have called attention to the rational white subject at the centre of the entire European Enlightenment project (Ladson-Billings, 2000; Smith, 1999), as well as the "male social universe" in which objective research takes place (Smith, 1974, p. 7). Postmodern and poststructural scholars have rejected the truth-claims and deterministic binaries (e.g., true/false) evident in quantitative designs (Usher, 1997). Further, many scholars have expressed alarm at "quantitative imperialism" (Bartels, 2004, p. 83)—the practice of quantitative methodologies being used by policy makers, funders, and ethics review committees as the gold standard against which all research is assessed (Brown & Strega, 2005; Denzin & Lincoln, 2005).

In a trans-specific context, critical discussion of the quantification of trans identities and bodies has quite recently deepened with a special issue of *Transgender Studies*

Quarterly (2015), devoted to a range of perspectives on "counting" trans individuals. In this issue, contributors debate whether quantification offers hope for equity in health and citizenship through "boxes of our own making" (Harrison-Quintana, Grant, & Rivera, 2015), or whether it paves the way for new forms of biopolitical state control (Currah & Stryker, 2015). Though the debate is far from settled, Singer (2015) suggests that we must move beyond the dichotomous view that locates resistance always on the outside of institutions and homogeneity always on the inside.

Overall, the critiques of quantitative methods cover much ground. Critiques have been aimed at the positivist stance (Denzin & Lincoln, 2005) and potential for state surveillance (Currah & Stryker, 2015) within quantitative methods specifically, at the power relations within traditional research irrespective of methodology (Potts & Brown, 2005), and at the modernist imperative of "truth seeking" evident in most methodologies (Strega, 2005). Among these various positions, quantitative research can be regarded as particularly emblematic of the problematic nature of traditional research (Strega, 2005). In social work and the practising professions, especially those claiming an anti-oppressive stance, these critiques index broader debates over "evidence-based practice" and the nature of the knowledge that ought to guide social interventions (Webb, 2001).

Let us first make clear that we do not dismiss these arguments. Emanating from established streams of scholarship, as well as from the knowledge and experience of groups on the margins, many of these critiques are well-founded and worthy of our attention. Yet we argue that in the emerging field of anti-oppressive research, these strands of critique can be brought together to prematurely foreclose possibilities for action. Indeed, within methodological debates, there is sometimes a tendency to impute particular characteristics onto researchers themselves. Denzin and Lincoln (2005) state that "qualitative researchers believe that rich descriptions of the social world are valuable, whereas quantitative researchers, with their etic, and nomothetic commitments, are less concerned with such detail" (p. 12). While there is certainly a trend toward considering the strengths of both designs (Mahoney & Goertz, 2006; Westmarland, 2001), political opposition to quantitative methods persists in the field and in the classroom.

We seek to trouble these broad brushstrokes by attending to the specificity of one project: Trans PULSE, which explored social exclusion and health among trans people in Ontario. With the community under study directing the selection of methodology, we take note that methodological choice is not always the sole domain of academic researchers. While not dismissive of critiques, we do suggest that these critiques might be descriptive of *much* quantitative research, rather than inherent to *all* quantitative research, and we ask if it is always the case that particular methodologies can have no place in social justice. Following Potts and Brown's (2005) assertion that anti-oppressive research is epistemologically distinct, rather than methodologically distinct, we outline the context from which our study emerged and the process by which community knowledge was kept at the forefront of our research design.

TRANS PEOPLE AND THE PROBLEM OF KNOWLEDGE

Salah (2009) remarks that contemporary trans people inherit an archive of problematic representations "rife with repudiation, pathologization and phantasy" (p. 1). The first scholarship referencing individuals whom we would today call trans emerged in 19th- and early 20th-century medicine, describing them as "psychopathic" deviants (Krafft-Ebing, 1877/2006). In the mid-20th century, the term *transsexual* came into use as a clinical field sprang up to study and "manage" these individuals (Meyerowitz, 2002). In the United States, university-based gender identity clinics were established to conduct research and determine access to newly developing "sex-change" procedures, which many desperately sought. Within these power relations, trans people hoping to improve their chances conferred with one another and consulted the clinical literature, with the result that clinicians' hypotheses were confirmed and reconfirmed by each new applicant performing the narrative of a "true" transsexual (Stone, 1996). Using these tautological "findings," clinicians dictated the acceptable dress, mannerisms, identities, and sexualities of those deemed eligible (see, for example, Green & Money, 1969). Though transsexuals actively negotiated with practitioners, over the latter half of the 20th century, their "self-appointed minders" (Stryker, 2006, p. 11) established an astonishing level of discursive and material control through their own clinical knowledge production. As Denny (1994) notes, their publications often displayed nothing short of contempt for trans people. While trans people were not completely without agency—they penned autobiographies and engaged the media (Meyerowitz, 2002)—their voices would not make it into academic speaking positions until the 1990s, coinciding with the introduction of the terms *transgender* and *trans* (Stryker, 2006).

Further compounding the problem of trans representation in clinical literature is the invisibility of trans people outside of this literature. Namaste (2000) developed the concept of *erasure*, which she described as "a condition which ultimately inscribes transsexuality as impossible" (pp. 4–5). Members of our research team (Bauer et al., 2009) identified two interrelated sites of erasure (informational and institutional erasure), noting that when trans people are not visible in informational systems (research studies, needs assessments, curricula, etc.), this in turn reinforces institutional erasure (i.e., the erasure of trans needs from the policies and practices of institutions). Indeed, the Canadian Census, the Canadian Community Health Survey, and all Statistics Canada surveys require the entry of information about sex/gender, yet do not provide any way to indicate that one is "transgender"—thus excluding trans people from the "national imaginary" (Currah & Stryker, 2015, p. 2). This pattern continues at the institutional level with the everyday forms and documents used to gather information for policy decisions.

Since services and policies are not created to accommodate people who do not exist, the concern is twofold: that trans people appear to exist in numbers so negligible that no public action is warranted on their behalf, and further, that any search for research about trans communities will unearth pathologizing texts numbering in the hundreds and perhaps thousands, with little information to illuminate community needs. Writing about trans people of colour in particular, Currah and Stryker (2015) note that given the high burden of poverty, violence, and HIV/AIDS borne by these individuals, the lack of state interest in documenting their health status indicates that they fall on the "let-die," rather than the "make-live," side of the biopolitical project (p. 5).

TRANSITION-RELATED CARE AND RESEARCH IN ONTARIO

Bauer (2012) notes that some of the most stigmatizing research on trans communities has come from Ontario. The theory of autogynephilia, advanced since the late 1980s by sexologist Ray Blanchard from the Centre for Addiction and Mental Health (CAMH) in Toronto (see Blanchard, 1985), has been criticized for dehumanizing trans women, limiting their access to transition care, and creating a false typology of trans women (Lane, 2008; Moser, 2009, 2010; Nuttbrock et al., 2011; Serano, 2010, 2015; Veale, 2015; Veale, Clark, & Lomax, 2008). The research and treatment model of the Child and Adolescent Gender Identity Service at CAMH (closed in 2015) has been criticized for pathologizing childhood gender variance and promoting conformity (Burke, 1996; Hird, 2003; Langer & Martin, 2004; Pickstone-Taylor, 2003; Pyne, 2014; Tosh, 2011a, 2011b; Wallace & Russell, 2013). Researchers from Toronto's CAMH played prominent roles in the American Psychiatric Association, chairing the DSM-IV and DSM-5 review committees for "sexual and gender identity disorders" (American Psychiatric Association, 2012; Bradley et al., 1991). Hundreds of publications advancing these theories have been circulated widely (Ansara & Hegarty, 2011). The CAMH centre in Toronto is also home to the long-contested (Adult) Gender Identity Clinic (Namaste, 2000).

While the (Adult) Gender Identity Clinic at CAMH has undergone recent changes that we understand many trans community members feel positively about, the central place of psychiatry/psychology within Ontario trans health care has been fraught. Prior to 1998, trans people hoping to be approved for transition-related health care (hormone therapy and surgical options) and to have these prohibitively expensive procedures funded by the Ontario Health Insurance Plan (OHIP) were required to present themselves for assessment and diagnosis at the Gender Identity Clinic. While not all trans people seek to medically transition, many do (Scheim & Bauer, 2015), and thus access to transition care has been and remains a strong focus of trans health activism. Namaste (2000) conducted the first research that sought to capture trans people's perspectives on this clinic, reporting the substantial contradiction between their health needs and the psychiatric assessment framework. With clinicians working within a narrow model of what constituted an "eligible" candidate, participant success was contingent on many factors beyond their control, most prominently their ability to pass a "Real Life Test" consisting of living full-time in their felt gender role for one to two years (including documented full-time employment) without the help of hormones or surgeries (Denny, 1992; Namaste, 2000). These and other gatekeeping criteria were often impossible to meet, and many trans people were denied care and funding (Denny, 1992).

Moreover, the research function of the clinic saw trans people serving as both patients and research subjects, a dual role that many who hoped to acquire approval were not in a position to decline (Namaste, 2000). Notably, the power relations that may have prevented trans people from exercising their right to refuse research consent are the same ones that may have impinged on the ability to be forthcoming about any life narrative that contradicted expectations. With a compromised research consent model and power relations that lacked the conditions for authentic speech, Namaste (2000) notes that not only was this an unacceptable model of health care, but it also called into question the validity of any research findings gathered in this context. Thus, trans communities have been understandably suspicious of research.

In 1998, the Ontario provincial government delisted sex-reassignment surgeries as OHIP-funded procedures, rendering even those candidates approved by the CAMH clinic ineligible to have their transition care covered. (Sex-reassignment surgery was re-listed in 2008 during the course of our project.) The burden of funding these expenses fell onto individuals. Unable to afford the approved procedures, many felt there was no longer a need to attend the clinic and thus the nature of the problems in trans health care began to shift. In the 1990s, the transgender movement in North America was gaining momentum and working to reframe trans people as a community, rather than a population with a shared mental health diagnosis (Stryker, 2006). With a broader range of identities becoming possible, the community was growing, yet lacked services to meet their needs.

In 2003, the explicitly trans-positive Sherbourne Health Centre (SHC) opened in Toronto and began to provide hormone therapy to trans people within a primary care model. The clinic quickly reached capacity, and while trans people from across the province were willing to drive long distances to receive care, the centre's catchment area was limited to Toronto. The most commonly cited statistic regarding the prevalence of trans people is 1 in 30,400 of those born female, and 1 in 11,900 of those born male (Bakker, van Kesteren, Gooren, & Bezemer, 1993), making for an estimated total of approximately 500 trans people in the entire province of Ontario. Yet SHC, as one clinic in one city, had approximately that number of trans patients, making it obvious that the trans community simply had to be larger than official statistics had ever captured. While the CAMH Gender Identity Clinic focused their research program on etiology and psychopathology, it became clear that research was required to document the growing size and diversity of the community and the extent of unmet needs. A number of qualitative trans health studies were published as grey literature reports in the late 1990s and early 2000s, laying the foundation for a larger study to document the scope of these needs in the broader policy arena (Gapka & Raj, 2003; Namaste, 1995).

THE TRANS PULSE PROJECT

The first conversations about a potential study took place in 2004 between two local trans service providers and a cisgender ally at SHC. Though research was needed, the broader context of power and knowledge production about trans lives meant that such a project might foster suspicion and fail, even with trans people involved. With this in mind, these individuals sought a small grant to build a research team, and, after selecting four community members through an open call for applications, the group sought academic partners. In a reversal of the typical community-based research relationship, a group made up of mostly trans community members interviewed potential researchers. Several researchers from a CAMH unit separate from the Gender Identity Clinic were interviewed, but due to some logistical incompatibilities, as well as a concern that association with CAMH could damage the project's reputation, this partnership did not move forward. One academic researcher who used primarily qualitative methods and another using primarily quantitative methods were chosen based on their expertise, their ability to secure funds, and their ability to be allies.

Issues of ethics, power, and process were forefront for our new team. In early conversations, we acknowledged that our ethical standards would likely exceed the typical protections of research ethics boards. For us, ethics included community accountability, such as ensuring that important results were made available quickly, in accessible formats. We agreed to appropriately contextualize potentially pathologizing findings, such as findings regarding mental illness or self-harm. Further, we committed to building the community's capacity for conducting their own research. Inspired by Indigenous Peoples' efforts to take control of research agendas in their communities, the team departed from the more limiting models of "community engagement" and "community participation," adopting instead a model of "community control." This model positioned the project as "owned" by trans communities, rather than by academic researchers. To this end, we developed a terms of reference document stipulating that the Investigators' Committee would be made up of a majority of trans community members and that for major decisions about the project to be made, a majority of the investigators present must be trans. We have written elsewhere about the challenges in operationalizing this stance of community control (Travers et al., 2013); however, we have remained committed to this framework throughout. At the team-building and qualitative stage (Phase I), funding was provided by the Wellesley Institute and the Ontario HIV Treatment Network. In the following survey stage (Phase II), funds were provided via multiple operating and dissemination grants from the Canadian Institutes of Health Research (CIHR), the Institute of Infection and Immunity, and the Institute of Gender and Health.

Phase I of Trans PULSE involved a series of qualitative "community soundings" (focus groups) across three Ontario cities. Trans communities are very diverse, and thus these soundings were designed to be inclusive of community members across race and ethnicity, class, Indigenous identity, sexual orientation, ability/disability, and immigration status. Soundings were also intended to welcome a range of trans individuals, including those who do and do not seek medical transition, spanning identities such as transsexual, transgender, transitioned, gender queer, and some Two-Spirit people. In total, 85 community members joined these soundings to recount unjust living conditions including poverty, employment and housing discrimination, and inability to access health and social services. Many shared their anger at being unable to afford or obtain approval for the gender-affirming procedures that would have made them less visible and vulnerable to discrimination and violence. They told us that they were often treated as mentally ill by service providers due to their trans identity, yet were simultaneously denied access to mental health services they felt they did require, sometimes as a result of their experiences as trans people. Due to their transgender status, many were refused access to gender-specific services such as shelters, rape crisis centres, and addictions treatment, yet again these were services many felt they required because of how they had been treated as trans people. Participants who sought health care were often unable to find knowledgeable or willing providers. As reported in one of our publications, one physician flatly said to a participant, "Please go somewhere else" (Bauer et al., 2009). Other participants reported avoiding health care altogether, due to the expectation of disrespect. In addition to these accounts, many participants articulated the sense that their existence was invisible. One participant said, "I'm one of the dead ones … all of this time that I've survived, I'm one of the walking dead because we're not counted; we're not represented anywhere" (Bauer et al., 2009). Participants urged facilitators to conduct a study to show the size of the community, in order to, as one participant put it, "put a pinprick in the balloon of these bullshit numbers that they're basing decisions on." This participant continued: "Until we blow that myth out of the water, we're only going to get funding that's based on a 1 in 30,000 of the population" (unpublished findings, 2009).

Selecting a Methodology

In considering which methodologies could accomplish participants' goals, we felt that given the dearth of local statistical information, policy makers would likely be most receptive to quantitative data. As Scout (2013) points out, findings from existing small community or regional trans health studies have not managed to have the impact of large-scale surveys. Yet we were also aware that the studies typically considered worthy of interest for health policy makers are those in which participants are chosen randomly, with findings therefore seen as more broadly generalizable than convenience sampling (Bryman, 2008). For many marginalized communities, no list of members exists, nor are groups such as trans people included in population counts, making adhering to a standard of random sampling impossible. While it is often assumed that methodological choice is the purview of academic researchers, in our case it was a community investigator who proposed respondent-driven sampling (RDS) as a solution to this problem.

RDS combines snowball sampling with a mathematical model to compensate for samples not selected randomly (Heckathorn, 2002). Recruitment begins with "seeds," initial participants who complete a survey and then invite a limited number of others to complete the survey as well, who in turn complete it and invite others. Through successive waves, an RDS sample begins to break from the characteristics of the initial participants and has been found to reach a wider cross-section of marginalized communities than other forms of recruitment (Ramirez-Valles et al., 2005). Participants' data are weighted based on the number of potential participants that they know, compensating for the fact that some people are highly connected to a community and thus more likely to be invited, whereas others are less connected and less likely to be invited (Heckathorn, 2002). This allows for results that are considered to be more "generalizable" than those from convenience samples. At a retreat, three community investigators and one academic researcher waded through the literature about RDS to understand its uses, limitations, and benefits. After considering the potential challenges of recruiting through a system of "invitations," a decision was made to use RDS in order to reach a broader range of trans people, demonstrate the size and diversity of the community, and produce findings we hoped would be taken seriously by policy makers.

Survey Design

In quantitative survey design, researchers must select what they will measure in advance, making it difficult to capture issues not previously anticipated (Bryman, 2008). Due to this limitation, our approach to survey design (Phase II) was to be as comprehensive as possible by rooting the process in community knowledge. At a weekend retreat, community investigators led a process of mapping out what they felt were the major issues in the community, based on their personal and professional experiences, as well as the findings from the Phase I community soundings. By this point in the project, we had put together a Community Engagement Team (CET)—16 trans advocates from across the province formed a committee of key advisors, and, along with investigators, they reviewed and provided feedback on successive survey drafts for over a year. In addition to geographic diversity, this team was composed of individuals who spanned a range of ages, gender identities, racial and ethnic identities, and identities as disabled, immigrant, or Indigenous Peoples. The diverse makeup of this team was intended to support our engagement with the diversity of individuals who would complete our survey (for a demographic breakdown, see Bauer, Travers, Scanlon, & Coleman, 2012). The CET team was also key to ensuring topics not usually covered in trans health studies, such as racism within trans communities, were adequately captured (see Longman Marcellin, Scheim, Bauer, & Redman, 2013). Though the resulting length of our survey (87 pages) defied all expert advice, community members felt that the community would be more offended by excluded topics than it would feel burdened by the length. In total, 23 community members drafted or gave input on survey questions. While it was challenging at times for community members to engage equally in what is typically an academic exercise (Travers et al., 2013), our collaborative process runs counter to the characterization of survey design as remote and removed from lived experience.

Data Collection

When it came time to launch, we endeavoured to make the survey accessible in multiple modes: online, on paper, and via telephone, with language interpreters if needed. We established a toll-free telephone line, a public email address, a Facebook group, and a survey website to communicate with potential participants. When recruitment proved challenging at first (due to frustration with waiting to be invited), some of our CET members created a YouTube video about the project (Huberdeau, 2009), and we held an in-person meeting with 40 trans community leaders in Toronto, as well as several conference calls with community leaders across Ontario. During these meetings, we shared preliminary data, explained the rationale for our methodology, and solicited feedback about the survey experience and what should be done with the findings. A year later, we had surveyed 433 respondents, the largest trans health study that had been conducted at that time in Canada.

Community Relevance and Impact

As analysis got underway, the emerging data corroborated many of the findings from our soundings, for example, high levels of poverty, discrimination, and unmet health needs. Yet survey data also differed in significant ways. Physical and sexual violence were not commonly spoken of in the soundings, yet survey data indicated these as pervasive experiences, with an estimated 20 percent of trans people having been physically or sexually assaulted for being trans (Bauer, Pyne, Francino, & Hammond, 2013). More striking, suicide was only briefly mentioned and did not emerge as a theme in the soundings, yet survey findings indicated that 77 percent had seriously considered suicide in their lifetime, and 43 percent had attempted (Bauer et al., 2013). It may be that the survey format provided an opportunity to share experiences that were too stigmatizing to voice in a group setting. It may also be that these numbers convey something distinct from—not more nor less important than—descriptive, lived experience.

Aiming for a wide range of audiences, we developed an extensive strategy for sharing our results. We released short e-bulletins to provide community members and service providers with findings that could be used for advocacy without the delays of the peer-review process or the subscription fees of journals. Since some key audiences included those who would give weight to the peer-review process (e.g., physicians and policy makers), open-access academic papers were targeted to specific publication forums. For example, we estimated that 21 percent of trans people reported that they had not gone to an emergency room at a moment when they needed emergency medical care, specifically because they were trans (Bauer, Scheim, Deutsch, & Massarella, 2014). Yet, to our knowledge, no article on trans people and emergency care had ever been published within emergency medicine literature. Hence we targeted an emergency medicine journal in the hope of reaching emergency department physicians. Cognizant that our team does not possess all the necessary community and disciplinary knowledge, we have co-authored papers with statisticians, prison activists, Indigenous community service providers, physicians, and others with relevant knowledge, many of whom are also trans community members. Aiming to return the data to trans communities, in 2012, we held a weekend-long Trans Health Advocacy Summit, during which we collaborated with 30 trans advocates from around the province to assess the provincial trans health situation and identify avenues for change.

Additionally, in the course of our work, a particular strength of our quantitative design has become apparent: Our large database is a resource that allows us to respond quickly to requests for information. For example, two youth-serving community agencies requested a report on the impact of parental support on the health and wellbeing of trans youth, resulting in some of our most powerful findings (Travers et al., 2012). The Canadian Human Rights Commission requested a rapid report on sex designations on identity documents (a major concern for many trans people), and these findings were used a week later in a committee meeting in the House of Commons. We were able to accommodate a request from the province's Ministry of Health and Long-Term Care for an estimate of unmet need for sex-reassignment surgeries in Ontario, and to produce requested data for the Gay Men's Sexual Health Summit and the Screening Saves Lives Program of the Canadian Cancer Society. When the province of Ontario re-listed sex-reassignment surgeries as OHIP-funded procedures in 2008, our findings were used in meetings with the Ministry of Health to advocate for improvements in the clinical settings where assessments would take place. Our findings were also used to launch a province-wide program of training in trans health care that continues to build capacity among Ontario primary health care and social service providers (Rainbow Health Ontario, 2013). Finally, our findings have been used in multiple court challenges on trans health issues and used by advocates in the Legislative Assembly of Ontario, the federal House of Commons, and the Canadian Senate in ongoing efforts to secure trans human rights protections.

MAKING TRANS PEOPLE COUNT: QUANTITATIVE METHODS AND SOCIAL JUSTICE RECONSIDERED

As noted, we have found a tendency within some anti-oppressive research literature to dismiss quantitative research methods and, at times, the researchers who employ those methods. Again, as noted, we accept the many well-founded critiques of mainstream methods and have endeavoured to write critically about the challenges in our project connected to our choice of method (Travers et al., 2013). Yet outright dismissals would seem to point to a failure to imagine agency, strategy, and context. Sedgwick and Frank (1995) maintain that, within critical theory, we must be self-reflexive about our "routines"—those critiques that are predictable and rote. Thus we question whether the dismissal of the social justice potential of particular research methodologies may be one such "routine" in anti-oppressive research, and we propose to reconsider methodological strategy in context.

In some critiques of quantitative methodologies, it has been said that the tools of the natural sciences cannot be usefully employed in the social world; that the quantification of social phenomena is outmoded for our complex milieu (Bryman, 2008). Yet in considering the context of Trans PULSE, we note the overwhelming absence of information about trans people and their needs, and the deleterious effects of those absences (Bauer et al., 2009; Scout, 2013). As scholars have pointed out, we can certainly view positivist-based methodologies as compliant with troubling power relations (Currah & Stryker, 2015). Yet in context, we may also view the mode of quantification as resistant to one of the ways that marginalization manifests and perpetuates itself in a trans-specific context: erasure. Indeed, *to be counted* is precisely what many participants in the qualitative portion of our study asked for. That we were able to surface descriptions of social violence through our community soundings was a major contribution; that we were able to answer questions of how much, how many, and how often was another.

In continuing to consider methodological choice in context, we also find the need to ask whether methods proposed as anti-oppressive always live up to this expectation. Strega (2005) rejects mainstream research methods as inconsistent with social justice goals, proposing instead a research paradigm that is a blend of poststructuralism and radical feminism. Yet, for trans communities, radical feminism has been responsible for some of the most aggressive forms of transphobia to appear in print, including numerous texts that have cast trans women as dangerous and jeopardized their access to vital women's services (see Daly, 1978; Greer, 1999; Raymond, 1979). Further, feminist poststructuralism, through the work of scholars such as Bernice Hausman (1995), has at times been used to undermine the legitimacy of trans people's identity narratives and their access to medical transition care. Thus, methodological consistency with social justice goals would seem to be highly context-specific.

As noted, the potential to have the ear of those who value research "rigour" was an important objective for Trans PULSE. To produce research that was "harder to dismiss" was indeed one of our stated goals. Yet, in neoliberal and austere times, we recognize that any research can be dismissed unless seen to contribute to increasing "efficiencies." Hoping that our findings would garner added authority due to our methodology, we took a risk, and so we have been heartened to see some success in this regard with our findings utilized in legislative lobbying, requested by policy makers, and published in disciplinary realms where trans health needs have never before been visible. Yet beyond our hoped-for impact on practitioners and policy makers, we find the quantification of injustice can have additional impacts. For example, at a recent conference for parents of transgender children, a father approached one of our investigators, sharing that one of our simple bar graphs depicting the profound impact of parental support on trans youth, including impacts on experiences of depression, health status, and suicidality (Travers et al., 2012), was the most powerful message he had encountered on his journey to support his child. Thus in our rush to debate methodological merit within our research texts, we run the risk of forgetting that marginalized people do not live out their lives in the pages of our texts.

In part, this discussion turns on the choice to engage or disengage with problematic relations, and to whom one imagines one is accountable to for that decision. Like Potts and Brown (2005), we observe the over-focus on impact within traditional research, to the neglect of a just and ethical research process. Indeed, we have attempted to attend to research process, particularly power relations, in unique ways (Travers et al., 2013). Yet we also observe an ethical contract with our participants, who asked us to make an impact on their behalf. Though it has been suggested that anti-oppressive researchers ought to reject mainstream methods, in our case it was members of the community under study who, after considering the benefits and flaws, proposed these methods as the most consistent with community goals. Though there will always be a danger in appealing to mainstream authority, in our current milieu, when scientific literature is relied upon for policy decisions that bear out on everyday lives, there is also a danger in abandoning the field of traditional research to those who have no commitment to social justice. We would argue, in fact, that mainstream engagement by anti-oppressive researchers is consistent with the tradition of anti-oppressive practitioners (in social work and other practising professions) to recognize the possibility of agency within institutional confines, and to respond strategically (Smith, 2007; Smith, this volume). Ultimately, we have chosen to treat the field of mainstream health research as a site to occupy, rather than vacate, and propose that anti-oppressive research stay attentive to the many possibilities for critical action.

2 | Anti-Oppression Qualitative Research Principles for Disability Activism

Reflections from the Field

Yahya El-Lahib, Assistant Professor, Faculty of Social Work, University of Calgary

History has given scholars many examples of how science, knowledge, and research have been used to marginalize and oppress social groups; through colonialism and dominance of Western and Eurocentric knowledge, certain social groups were othered, marginalized, and oppressed (Denzin & Lincoln, 2005; Potts & Brown, 2005; Quijano, 2000, 2008; Ristock & Pennell, 1996; Rossiter, 2000; Smith, 1999; Strega, 2005). In fact, Quijano (2000) asserts that controlling knowledge production served as the most effective tool to maintain Eurocentric hegemony and allowed for Europe's domination. In contrast to this history, authors such as Brown and Strega (2005), Potts and Brown (2005), Ristock and Pennell (1996), herising (2005), and Rossiter (2000), as well as Strega (2005), argue for the use of research as a tool for resistance and empowerment of marginalized groups and communities. Indeed, Brown and Strega (2005) insist that "research from the margins is not research on the marginalized but research by, for, and with them/us" (p. 7). In this chapter, I explore the potential that anti-oppressive research principles can provide to marginalized communities in ways that help negotiate power dynamics and relations during the research process and leading up to its outcomes and dissemination.

The discussion in this chapter is illustrated with examples from my practice and research experiences as a disability activist in Lebanon, a global South country. Throughout my experience, I have witnessed how research can be used to oppress, as well as to resist social injustice. Yet there is a gap in the qualitative research methodology scholarship that focuses on the research issues involved in conducting studies on disability rights in global South contexts. Indeed, Barker and Murray (2010), Chataika (2012), Groce (2005), Ghai (2001, 2012), Grech (2011, 2012), and Goodley and Lawthom (2011), as well as Holden and Beresford (2002), note that even within the critical disability research scholarship, the emphasis has been on global North contexts, with a clear gap in methodologies and substantive topics being applied to global South contexts and realities. While the critical disability research scholarship emphasizes the need for research that works toward ending the marginalization of people with disabilities (e.g., Barnes & Mercer, 2006; Moore, Beazley, & Maelzer, 1998), the field has been dominated by Northern scholarship (Barnes & Mercer, 2003; Barker & Murray, 2010; Goodley, Hughes, & Davis, 2012; Grech, 2011, 2012; Wehbi, 2011). Chataika (2012) does not call for dismissing this scholarship; instead, she argues for the need for genuine collaborations and inclusion of scholarship and critical disability research agendas from the global South to reverse the "colonial legacy" (p. 259) that manifests itself through the assumed universality of dominant knowledges and scholarship produced in the global North.

Similarly, Grech (2012) calls for critical global disability studies, a project that aims to respond to the "imperialistic trail of western knowledge and practices" (p. 52) that dominates disability studies in a way that homogenizes, generalizes, simplifies, and ignores disability knowledge and theorization from the global South. The author asserts that such a project aims to "decolonize" thought and epistemologies and contributes to making a place for "marginalized and disaccredited knowledges" (p. 66) informed by thinkers, activists, and the experiences of people from the global South. Such an understanding has the potential to revalue marginalized ways of knowing by critically centring North/South power dynamics and relations; doing so contributes to the resistance role that anti-oppression research seeks to represent and embody.

Before moving forward, it is important to note that this chapter is situated within a critical understanding of colonialism, its history, and its contemporary manifestations, and adopts the concepts of global North and South to refer to the unjust colonial divisions that perpetuate unbalanced cultural, economic, and socio-political power dynamics and relations (Bush, 2006; Loomba, 2005). Hence, within this understanding, I contend that the global South is not a homogeneous socio-political, economic, and geographic reality. Instead, it is a way to highlight and acknowledge the complex colonial power relations and dynamics within, and between, both hemispheres. Such acknowledgement situates the discussion in ways that centre the colonial binaries between the global North and South, within which the assumed superiority and universality of knowledges produced in the global North not only becomes apparent but is also questioned and challenged. Thus, in this chapter, the terms *global North* and *global South* are not meant to homogeneously construct these geographic entities. Instead, they serve as a way to critically examine the power relations that exist as a result of these binaries and to demonstrate their impacts on the legitimization of certain knowledges over others.

To contextualize the above discussion, in this chapter, I explore the potential of applying qualitative anti-oppressive research principles to disability issues in global South contexts. I will argue that there is potential for qualitative anti-oppressive research to contribute to challenging marginalization and enhancing the work of disability movements seeking social justice. Brown and Strega (2005) note that even though much has been written about critical social research methodologies, anti-oppressive research principles have not been "well understood" (p. 4) and are thus marginalized in the research methodology scholarship. My hope in this chapter is to contribute to elucidating the potential usefulness of these principles for research, especially to support social justice. Relying on my long history of research and practice experience with disability organizations in Lebanon and Canada, I will explore this argument through a discussion of anti-oppressive qualitative research principles. Throughout this discussion, I will focus on the research process and outcomes and explore the notions of contextuality, voice and representation, relationship-building, and positionality to demonstrate the actual and potential contributions of anti-oppression research principles for social justice–oriented research. In addition, I rely on examples from my own practice experience to engage in self-reflexivity about my role as a researcher in order to demonstrate the potential contributions of anti-oppressive research to the fields of social work and critical disability studies.

ANTI-OPPRESSIVE RESEARCH: KEY TENETS AND PRINCIPLES

Qualitative anti-oppressive research is committed to a political purpose, and it encourages researchers and the communities they work with to actively participate in seeking social change to ensure the inclusion of all marginalized and oppressed social groups, such as people with disabilities (Moosa-Mitha, 2005; Potts & Brown, 2005). Critical disability scholars such as Dossa (2006, 2009), Linton (1998), Meekosha (2011), Vazquez (2011), and Withers (2012) argue that people with disabilities have been oppressed through their marginalization and exclusion from full participation in societies. For example, people with disabilities are marginalized through institutions and other exclusionary policies that limit their participation in important areas such as the educational system and in the workforce (Turmusani, 2003; Vazquez, 2011). This is further seen in social research and practices that have adopted a medical model (Cameron, 2007; Grech, 2009). As a result, people with disabilities are excluded and become invisible in mainstream society to the extent that decisions that directly impact their lives are made *for* them and not *by* them (Flower & Wirz, 2000; Yeo & Moore, 2003). This has been equally true in research, as several critical disability scholars have noted (Barnes & Mercer, 2006; Chataika, 2012; Ghai, 2012; Goodley & Lawthom, 2011; Moore, Beazley, & Maelzer, 1998; Nind, 2011; Seymour, 2001).

In contrast to exclusionary research practices, anti-oppressive research allows researchers and researched social groups to have an equitable and mutual relationship, in which the voices of marginalized groups could be heard (Brown & Strega, 2005; Potts & Brown, 2005). Potts and Brown (2005) note three main tenets of anti-oppressive research: "Anti-oppressive research is resistance in process and in outcome" (p. 60); "anti-oppressive research recognizes that all knowledge is socially constructed and political" (p. 61); and "the anti-oppressive research process is all about power and relationships" (p. 62). Relying on these tenets, I will focus my discussion on methodological principles related to the importance of context, the role of the researcher and researched community, the research process, and research outcomes.

As noted earlier, I have been involved in the resistance efforts of disability rights organizations, including conducting research to support advocacy initiatives to transform Lebanese society to become more inclusive of people with disabilities. In this sense, research has been used to counteract the invisibility and marginalization experienced by people with disabilities in public spheres. As an example, I was involved in a research project that examined the educational experiences and requirements of people with disabilities in a rural area of Lebanon, with the express aim of using the findings to contest institutionalization and challenge obstacles to inclusion within the educational system (Wehbi & El-Lahib, 2007a). Another example is a research project, also in a rural area, that aimed to identify the structural barriers preventing the inclusion of people with disabilities in the mainstream labour market (Wehbi & El-Lahib, 2007b). These examples are a reflection of Moosa-Mitha's (2005) argument that anti-oppressive research and "theories offer an analysis of social reality and a vision of social justice" (p. 61).

The above studies highlight how anti-oppressive research can help in exploring and understanding realities, challenging the unbalanced power dynamics, advancing a social inclusion agenda, and reversing the history of marginalization that people with disabilities face. The outcomes of both studies were used in community reports, in the design of advocacy campaigns, and in policy development. As importantly, the process of research was initiated and implemented by activists with disabilities with the assistance of academic researchers–activists. This process allowed the activists with disabilities not only to voice their concerns and design the research accordingly but also to engage in a learning process about research and to contribute their knowledge of the issues affecting their lives to the research process and outcomes.

IMPORTANCE OF CONTEXTUALITY

Within anti-oppressive qualitative research, it is important to understand the specific local socioeconomic and political context of oppression and exclusion of people with disabilities when conducting research. Specifically, it is critical not to assume that the knowledge gained from studies done in the global North with people with disabilities reflects the realities or experiences of people with disabilities in a global South country such as Lebanon. This assumed universality of knowledge produced in the global North can be traced back to North/South power relations perpetuated by colonial history and enforced through neocolonialism, international development, and international institutions such as the International Monetary Fund and the World Bank

(Barker & Murray, 2010; Chataika, 2012; Connell, 2007, 2011; Dingo, 2007; Ghai, 2012; Grech, 2009, 2011, 2012; McEwan, 2009; Meekosha, 2011).

Chataika (2012) asserts that for research to be "meaningful," especially in supporting development efforts, local actors need to be actively involved beyond merely consultation. Pe-Pua (1989) adds that research needs to resist this universalization of knowledge and needs to adapt to, or come from, the specific context within which it is being conducted. While Schreiber (2000) argues against ethnocentrism and Eurocentricity in intercultural research, which marginalizes and ignores the cultural perspectives and socio-historical realities of people in non-Northern contexts, Smith (1999) rejects the use of "universal" knowledge because it is a way to "legitimate the imposition of colonial rule" (p. 63). Thus, for anti-oppressive research to be meaningful and not to reproduce dominance and marginalization, it has to be rooted within the local realities and pay particular attention to the local socioeconomic and political contexts within which research is taking place.

Specifically, within global South contexts, an understanding of the impacts of colonialism and/or the dominance of Northern knowledge needs to be taken into account when conducting research. For example, in her discussion of the assumed universality of dominant Northern knowledges, Chataika (2012) offers a comprehensive critique of international development practices that reinforce the colonial process of homogeneity in the continent of Africa. Specifically, the author rejects the influence global North international development agencies and researchers have on disability knowledge production and legitimization and calls for a collaborative research relationship "where parties are equal, and where differences are used as learning moments to benefit both parties" (p. 255). In the same vein, Grech (2012) contends that "disability studies becomes complicit in the neocolonising" of the global South if it does not question and challenge the dominance of Western disability knowledge, theories, and practices (p. 52). Indeed, as alluded to earlier, such a challenge would make space for marginalized knowledges to be shared and benefited from.

However, taking the local context into account has not always been the case in terms of research. For example, in Lebanon, I witnessed how discourses and terminologies developed in the global North were used, applied, and legitimized by local actors because they were favoured and imposed by foreign backers. Certainly, this development is not unique to the Lebanese context. For example, in her discussion of disability rights activism, Ghai (2001) notes this phenomenon in India. This imposed use of language impacts how issues of marginalization and exclusion are negotiated and communicated locally in research and practice.

A concrete example concerns the widespread use, in Lebanon, of the term *persons with special needs*, developed in a Northern context. This problematic term depoliticizes and individualizes the experience of disability and focuses on impairment. Speaking of the development and prevalence of the term *special* in Northern contexts, Linton (1998) argues it is reflective of paternalistic attitudes toward people with disabilities. However, it is this paternalistic term that may have led to the rejection of the Arabic equivalent of the term *people with disabilities*, which has been politicized by the disability rights movement in Lebanon because it places the emphasis on the contextual elements that lead to disabling conditions such as social and structural barriers. As Linton (1998) notes, the term *disabled people* refers to a "group bound by common social and political experiences" and used to define and join people for political and collective activism (p. 12). I would contend that the use of depoliticized terms within Southern contexts stems from a specific "mainstreaming" ideology influenced by Western discourses on disability promoted by international institutions such as the World Bank (Dingo, 2007; Ghai, 2001; Grech, 2009; Meekosha, 2011).

RESEARCH PROCESS: REPRESENTATION, RELATIONSHIPS, AND POSITIONALITY

Anti-oppressive social work practice and research encourage us—practitioners and researchers—to work *with*, not *for*, marginalized and oppressed social groups. In her discussion of key elements of Indigenous epistemology, Kovach (2005) argues that the relationship between researcher and research participants is a "natural part of the research methodology" (p. 28). Lavallée (2009) adds that this should be "a lifelong relationship and commitment" (p. 24). Therefore, it is important when conducting research from an anti-oppressive approach to build a relationship between researcher and researched groups that goes beyond simply collecting data or conducting a study. Indeed, there is a body of literature that emphasizes and argues for the importance of relationship-building between the researcher and researched communities (e.g., herising, 2005; Kovach, 2005; Moosa-Mitha, 2005; Potts & Brown, 2005).

Recognizing the importance of building relationships in anti-oppressive research requires the researcher and the researched community to be upfront about limitations, obstacles, tensions, and challenges they may face, as well as opportunities that the research may present. Being upfront would contribute to building an equitable research relationship as opposed to a top-down one, where knowledge has traditionally been owned by the researcher and where the researched community has only been the "subject" of study (Smith, 1999). These types of inequitable research relationships have reinforced oppression as in the example of Indigenous Peoples, who have been the subject of research studies that were used to justify their assumed "inferiority" and the need for "civilizing" them by the colonizers (Adams, 1999, p. 8). This history has led to the need to adopt decolonizing Indigenous research paradigms that challenge the dominance of Eurocentric worldviews and methodologies (Baskin, 2011; Hart, 2002; Kovach, 2005; Lavallée, 2009). Specifically, for Indigenous researchers, this history means the need to take control and be aware of the "power politics of knowledge" (Kovach, 2005, p. 23). Kovach maintains that if knowledge is the vehicle to understand and establish societal values, then controlling its production is an essential component of cultural survival. Similarly, Baskin (2005b), Lavallée (2009), and Smith (1999) note that adopting decolonizing Indigenous research paradigms ensures the participation and voices of Indigenous Peoples are heard and their experiences recognized as a form of resistance.

Similarly, as Barnes and Mercer (1997); Goodley, Hughes, and Davis (2012); and Withers (2012) assert, the context of oppression of people with disabilities has historically led to research being done about them without their active and equitable participation. Indeed, people with disabilities have been subjected to top-down research that has been done about them instead of them being part of setting the overall research agenda (Chataika, 2012). A key contribution of anti-oppressive research is that it helps in facilitating and negotiating power dynamics and relationships between all parties involved in the research process. As such, the research relationship between the researchers and researched communities allows for the aims and purposes of research to be negotiated upfront and to be maintained throughout the research process, leading to its outcomes and dissemination. In other words, being active participants in the research process could challenge the hierarchical nature of the research relationship and allows researched groups and communities to be present in the research process and outcomes, as was the case in the previously mentioned research projects about education and employment.

Such a process ensures that the research relationship–building process is not only a lasting one, but also acknowledges actual and potential contributions to social justice in the research process and outcomes. In other words, investing in relationship building in research not only ensures an equitable relationship that shapes the research process but also guides such a process to eventually lead to research outcomes that are relevant to all parties involved. In my experiences in the aforementioned studies, relationship-building guided the process from the inception of research ideas, through defining the objectives and purpose of the research, conducting the studies, and to communicating findings, including how these would be used to advance the resistance agenda of the disability movement on the issues examined. Throughout this process, emergent issues and concerns were discussed and negotiated in transparent and reflexive ways to maintain a research agenda that was defined and controlled by disability activists to advance the political aims that motivated conducting these studies in the first place.

Furthermore, recognizing the researcher's social location and positionality within the broader context and in relation to the researched community is vital when conducting research (Langhout, 2006; Ristock & Pennell, 1996). As herising (2005) argues, an important element of critical research with marginalized social groups is to "interrogate and challenge the various fields of power, authority, and privilege that are embodied and practiced by the researcher" (p. 133). Langhout (2006) adds that while we cannot eliminate power differences between researchers and researched communities, it is important to be aware of power relations and our personal social location and identities because they play into the research process and outcomes. For example, in her study with racialized women with disabilities, Dossa (2006) invites researchers to recognize and be aware of unequal power relations in research through the use of reflexivity. The author argues that being reflexive would help researchers minimize appropriation of the voices of participants and to highlight inequalities within the research process and outcomes. (For more discussion about the critical role of reflexivity and its contributions to anti-oppressive research, please see Silver, this volume.) Hence, being reflexive would help researchers position themselves in a way that recognizes how they are part of the overall context within which research is taking place (Moosa-Mitha, 2005).

In my experience, when conducting research with disability rights organizations in Lebanon, it has been crucial to be reflexive and to be aware of my positionality. Although I do have various impairments and limitations, I have never been socially constructed as an individual with disability. This is not the place to elaborate on these tensions; however, I use this example here to demonstrate the complexities and nuances of identities and their influence on the research process and outcome. Hence, as a nondisabled researcher, I have become aware that I could never really understand the marginalization experiences of people with disabilities. In addition, this has meant that I need to be aware of my power and influence and that I cannot impose my own interpretation of these experiences. Instead, working with the community as a researcher has helped me to become an ally who is part of a movement that is seeking political and social transformation to challenge marginalization and ensure the rights of people with disabilities.

Furthermore, as a nondisabled researcher, I have been exposed to situations where ableism has played a role in how I was perceived by the broader society as being the expert because of my perceived privileges. Because of my construction as a nondisabled researcher, other researchers or practitioners would direct their discussion about issues of disability to me, instead of discussing the issue with my colleagues who have disabilities and who are long-time activists and well-known leaders, not only within the disability movement but in broader society. These realities are not specific to disability research contexts in Lebanon. For example, in her study with women who are mental health service recipients, Gray (2007) discusses the importance of challenging the oppressive role that the researcher has historically played; she argues for the importance of encouraging women in her study to voice their stories using their own words. The author adds that this allowed participants to be "both the producers and distributors of their voices" (p. 412). As such, it has been important for me to be reflexive about my social location and to situate myself within the broader context of oppression to prevent or avoid situations where I am seen to represent people with disabilities. Representing people with disabilities would give me "power over" as opposed to "power together" (Tew, 2006, pp. 36, 38); the latter involves recognizing that it is people with disabilities who can best represent themselves and that I have a role to play in working with them as an ally to achieve this goal.

In addition, as a nondisabled researcher situated within an overall context of oppression of people with disabilities, I have had to be aware of the "politics of location" (herising, 2005). Specifically, I witnessed how decisions are made for people with disabilities by their families. For example, I worked on a study where I interviewed people with disabilities in their homes (Wehbi & El-Lahib, 2007a). Within Lebanese cultural gender norms, especially in a rural context, being a male researcher meant that my interviews with women participants always involved the presence of a family member. In such situations, while conducting the interviews, I frequently had to intervene with parents who would attempt to respond on behalf of the family members with disabilities with whom I was conducting the interview. I had to intervene to ensure confidentiality and to hear the experiences of women with disabilities speaking in their own voices and on their own behalf.

This example may seem to pose some challenges to confidentiality and ethics, especially in terms of gender dynamics. However, in one particular instance, I was allowed to conduct the interview despite being a male because of the trust relationship that the family had established with the disability movement, which allowed them to feel comfortable with me interviewing their daughter. The issue here is twofold. First, the trust relationship that had been built with the family and the disability movement allowed me to navigate my relationship in the research process with confidence that the research would contribute to advancing the resistance agenda that the family supported. Second, the interventions I had to make constantly during the interview are related to dominant conceptions of people with disabilities as dependent even within their families; this perception of dependency gave family members permission to respond to questions directed to their daughter. However, as argued throughout this chapter, it is important to judge these examples with an understanding that challenges the Eurocentric and Western understanding of research, ethics, and confidentiality and not assume that they should be universal and applicable to global South contexts and realities.

RESEARCH OUTCOMES: RESISTING DOMINANT POWER RELATIONS

What is the purpose of doing research if we are not challenging power relations that reinforce the oppressive status quo? In responding to this question, I am trying to emphasize the importance of anti-oppressive research in giving voice to those who are not heard, to include those who are excluded, and to work toward social justice. As Fine (2006) notes, an important question for anti-oppressive research is how we can use studies "to provoke a greater awareness of injustice and to contribute to social movements more intimately" (p. 83). Thus, the purpose of conducting research for an activist is political and not simply an academic exercise of trying to reach "truth and knowledge as ends in themselves" (Humphrey, 2007, p. 14). From an anti-oppressive perspective doing qualitative research is about ensuring that research outcomes become the tools to challenge injustice.

In other words, the outcomes of qualitative anti-oppressive research should be applied to everyday experiences of people with disabilities, and not just remain knowledge owned by the researcher and geared toward specific audiences (e.g., academics or other researchers) in a way that does not reach activists with disabilities or challenge the marginalization of people with disabilities. Within anti-oppression research, the processes of conducting the research are as important as their outcomes, in the sense that they reflect a commitment to living anti-oppression values and principles through creating a space of inclusion and participation within research (Brown & Strega, 2005; herising, 2005; Potts & Brown, 2005). As such, the anti-oppressive research process becomes a building block of a broader social justice agenda that seeks to challenge the marginalization of people with disabilities.

For example, in my activism experience, research about people with disabilities has been used as a tool to expand knowledge about the realities of people with disabilities to challenge oppression. This is especially relevant within a local context where people with disabilities have been marginalized and rendered invisible. Furthermore, the need to use research outcomes to challenge oppression is ever necessary when taking into account the broader context of global North/South power relations, where knowledge production has worked to reinforce oppressive, unbalanced power relations between global North and global South. Taking this context into account, Chataika (2012), Ghai (2012), and Sherry (2007) argue for the need to include the history of colonialism in understanding the experiences of people with disabilities in the global South. Ghai asserts that such an analysis would allow for an "understanding of the Other, historically and symbolically" (2012, p. 273), which can potentially help in better understanding issues of identity, representation, and marginalization faced by people with disabilities. Hence, the outcomes of anti-oppressive research within global South contexts could be used to resist marginalization. In my experience, research outcomes have been used to strategize for future advocacy campaigns that sought the inclusion of people with disabilities in areas such as education, employment, and political rights, while taking into account the specific historical and contemporary realities of power relations locally and globally (Wehbi & El-Lahib, 2007a, 2007b, 2008). In addition, research has been undertaken by the disability rights organizations I have been involved with to highlight the absence of people with disabilities from decision making and to propose alternatives that promote their participation and inclusion.

Finally, anti-oppressive qualitative research could provide researchers and communities with alternatives to the traditional quantitative scientific criteria of validity and reliability that are at the centre of quantitative positivist research (Padgett, 2008; Tracy, 2010). Instead of focusing on such criteria, qualitative anti-oppressive research allows researchers the openness to use other ways of evaluating the worth of a study. For example, in action research, the action that was created through the process of the study and whether a problem that had been identified has been resolved are the "key criteria" to evaluate a study (Sandleowski, 2004, p. 1371). The author adds that, in critical forms of action research, an important criterion by which to evaluate a study is whether it has contributed to undermining oppression. Here, Sandleowski (2004) maintains that qualitative research findings could be evaluated based on whether they provide participants with the opportunity to better understand their own experiences.

Similarly, from an anti-oppressive research perspective, research relevance and worth can be evaluated based on whether studies achieve the aims of challenging injustice (Potts & Brown, 2005). Indeed, the studies I have been involved with as part of the disability rights movement in Lebanon may not be seen as reliable or valid from a positivist framework, perhaps due to small sample sizes, but they have certainly been effective in contributing to policy change for the rights of people with disabilities in areas such as education and employment, as noted earlier. This is consistent with Potts and Brown's (2005) discussion of measuring research credibility where anti-oppressive research is more concerned with "theoretical" and "principled" (p. 277) questions than with measuring technicality of the research such as validity and reliability. For example, the study on barriers to mainstream education led directly to the development of policy change, advocacy demands, and teacher-training programs. These studies have also provided people with disabilities with the opportunity to reframe their own experiences in ways that help them not just to better understand the oppression that they are facing but also to locate social and structural barriers and to identify ways to challenge them. Judged on this basis, these studies could be seen as significant and worthwhile pieces of research that have the potential to challenge oppression and marginalization and to contribute to social transformation.

CONCLUSION

In this chapter, I discussed anti-oppressive qualitative research with a focus on people with disabilities and disability issues in the global South. Specifically, I argued that relying on an anti-oppressive approach allows us to challenge power relations within the research process, outcomes, and research relationship between the researcher and researched communities. Based on my own research experiences within the disability rights movement in Lebanon, I provided examples of how contextuality, reflexivity, positionality, and relationship-building are vital to take into account within qualitative anti-oppressive research. I also discussed the important use of research outcomes to advance the rights of people with disabilities, which is possible when adopting an anti-oppressive research approach. Throughout this discussion, I explored how adopting an anti-oppressive framework when conducting social work research can help in challenging power relations, and in advancing social and political agendas that challenge marginalization and seek equity and social justice.

Research could be used to oppress and marginalize social groups and to create power divisions between people based on their identities and belonging. The important contribution that anti-oppressive research makes is the shifting of research from its oppressive uses toward a more politicized research that concerns itself with contributing to achieving equity and social justice. The researcher has an important role to play in ensuring that knowledge is gained through a mutual and equitable relationship and not by subjecting people to research only in order to arrive at a "truth" or to develop theories. Knowing the history of research and the ways it has been used to oppress social groups, I believe that anti-oppression research principles hold the seeds to advance a social justice agenda and resist the marginalization of people with disabilities both locally and globally.

3 | Critical Arts-Based Research

An Effective Strategy for Knowledge Mobilization and Community Activism

Purnima George,[1] *Associate Professor, School of Social Work, Ryerson University*

Critical and anti-oppressive social work research is premised on the notion that research has political purpose and has the potential to galvanize communities for addressing societal injustices and inequities (Ellwood, Thorpe, & Coleman, 2013; Kincheloe, McLaren, & Steinberg, 2011; Potts & Brown, 2005). Knowledge mobilization is a significant aspect of such research as it entails bringing together multiple stakeholders—community members, practitioners, policy makers, and other decision-makers—for influencing policies and practices (Bennet & Bennet, 2008; Bussières et al., 2008; Clover & Craig, 2009). For that reason, developing effective knowledge mobilization strategies becomes an integral aspect of research process (Briggs et al., 2015).

While the available literature provides templates for developing knowledge mobilization strategies and describes the different approaches, many of these strategies are researcher-driven and feature low levels of community engagement in effecting change (Briggs et al., 2015). These strategies fall short of the basic tenets of critical and anti-oppression research, which believes that the community has agency (Reitsma-Street & Brown, 2004); that all knowledge is oriented toward social justice and resistance in process and in outcome; that knowledge is socially constructed and political; and that the research process is all about power and relationships (Potts & Brown, 2005). Grounded within the beliefs of critical and anti-oppression research, this chapter reflects on my experiences with regard to knowledge mobilization in the context of a community action research project.

KNOWLEDGE MOBILIZATION

The literature on research dissemination presents a number of terms including *dissemination, knowledge transfer, knowledge exchange,* and *knowledge mobilization.* Dissemination, knowledge transfer, and knowledge exchange are practices that are unidirectional in nature and presuppose a transfer of information from a researcher to practitioners and other stakeholders in the research (Broner, Franczak, Dye, & McAllister, 2001; Bussières et al., 2008). This perspective assumes only experts such as researchers possess knowledge. It also assumes knowledge exists only in empirical form and is transferred through a top-down process. Therefore, any problems that arise in the application of knowledge into practice are attributed to stakeholders' lack of capacity (Broner et al., 2001). This view does not fit well with the critical and anti-oppression research that believes that knowledge is socially constructed and political.

Bennet and Bennet (2008) describe knowledge mobilization as "collaborative entanglement"; knowledge mobilization allows people to purposely and consistently develop and support approaches and processes that combine the sources of knowledge and the beneficiaries of that knowledge to interactively move toward a common direction (p. 48). This understanding of knowledge mobilization emphasizes social interaction and the collaborative nature of knowledge creation. Scholars have also stressed the underlying purpose of knowledge mobilization is to make an intellectual, social, and economic impact on the larger society (Felt, Rowe, & Curlew, 2004; Jacobson, Ochocka, Wise, & Janzen, 2007). Within this overall understanding of knowledge mobilization, there are varying perspectives among scholars.

Phipps, Johnny, and Zanotti (2009) view knowledge mobilization as a method that encompasses a collection of services developed to enhance the connection between researchers and stakeholders to influence practices and policies. On the other hand, the knowledge mobilization working group Activating Change Together for Community Food Security (ACT for CFS; 2014) visualizes knowledge mobilization within the context of participatory action research (PAR) as a process wherein researchers and community members co-construct knowledge through iterative processes.

Some scholars have identified core principles that guide knowledge mobilization. First, according to Baumbusch and colleagues (2008), knowledge is "dynamic, complex and socially constructed" (p. 133). Those scholars note the continual process of knowledge co-creation enables knowledge to be contextually relevant. Furthermore, some scholars have discussed the different types of knowledge and their contribution. Habermas (1972) has identified three types of knowledge: instrumental or traditional scientific knowledge that is expert driven; interactive knowledge that is gained from people's experiences; and critical knowledge that is grounded in reflective thinking and action. According to the ACT for CFS (2014), in knowledge mobilization within PAR, all the three types of knowledge are synthesized for taking action for change.

Second, in order for knowledge mobilization to be effective, the research must be relevant to communities' social issues, and the resulting knowledge must help to address those issues (Baumbusch et al., 2008). These scholars have spoken about the importance of timely research questions and activities that bring together various stakeholder groups for action.

Third, strong relationships are key to effective knowledge mobilization (Levin, 2008). In order to use the research findings to effect practice-based or policy changes, researchers must establish good working relationships built on trust and mutual respect with stakeholders and community members.

Fourth, effective knowledge mobilization depends on the engagement of all research stakeholders in an ongoing learning process (CIHR, 2004). Scholars have discussed the importance of stakeholders' active participation during all stages of research and particularly when research findings are being used to address local social issues.

Fifth, taking action on the knowledge generated through research requires capacity building. The lack of capacity to convert research findings into action could result in a loss of useful knowledge. Besides developing capacities, Levin (2008) and Lavis (2006) also discuss the importance of supports such as infrastructure, relationships, and networks as critical elements to support knowledge mobilization activities.

Sixth, knowledge mobilization strategies should be adaptable and multidisciplinary. The strategies must align with the diverse background of the stakeholders who are likely to use the research findings. In situations where researchers are dealing with complex issues, their knowledge mobilization strategies should incorporate multiple perspectives and multiple action plans that could result in the desired change (CIHR, 2004).

Finally, any effective knowledge mobilization effort should be holistic, far-reaching, and long-lasting in nature. Since changes may happen over a long period of time, Levin (2008) recommends that many evidences be developed to support the work of practice and policy change. A single piece of evidence, for example, may not create enough pressure for change. For that reason, it is important to develop knowledge mobilization strategies that have a long-term focus.

Scholars who support knowledge mobilization have also spoken about the necessity of a planned strategy. While the literature does not provide a set formula for a successful knowledge mobilization strategy, it does provide a list of factors that need to be considered while developing such a strategy. According to Briggs and colleagues (2015), a knowledge mobilization strategy must take into account the following factors: the context within which research is taking place; the nature of research findings; the nature of expected outcomes; the stakeholders who will be most affected by the findings; the stakeholders who have the power to make decisions; and the various stakeholder groups' expected level of engagement. These factors will be discussed in greater detail within the context of critical arts as a strategy of knowledge mobilization.

THE RESEARCH STUDY AND ITS KNOWLEDGE MOBILIZATION

Together with a Toronto-based social service agency that serves older adults, I conducted a Community Action Research (CAR) study. An increasing number of older adults from nearby neighbourhoods had approached the agency for material supports. Due to insufficient information about this particular issue, the agency planned to conduct a study to explore older adults' living conditions and the factors that led to material deprivation, and to obtain older adults' recommendations to effect change. In light of the social justice and social change focus of the research (Reitsma-Street & Brown, 2004; St. Denis, 2004), I discussed the suitability of using CAR with the agency's staff members and then proceeded to initiate the project.

As a part of the CAR process, community partners and leaders and older adults who were known to the agency were invited to participate in a meeting. At this meeting, a research advisory committee (RAC) was formed. The RAC validated the agency's observations and approved the two neighbourhoods that had been chosen as research sites. The selection of neighbourhoods was based on the fact that there was a large number of immigrant families with older adults living in poverty in those neighbourhoods (Boston, 2009; City of Toronto, 2006a, 2006b).

Over time, contacts in both communities were established by going to places visited regularly by older adults, such as places of worship, local businesses, and other social service agencies. Additional contacts were also made with social and religious networks of men and women and by visiting the rental buildings in which older adults resided.

Data collection was initiated after three to four months, when sufficient rapport had been established between the older adults and members of the research team, which was composed of myself, agency staff members, and community volunteers. Pe-Pua (1989) and St. Denis (2004) have spoken about the importance of rapport with research participants during data collection. The data were gathered through a number of community dialogues that honoured the communities' relational ways of knowing and sharing knowledge. Chilisa (2012) has spoken about the importance of doing data collection in ways that are consistent with communities' ways of knowing and sharing. The dialogues were conducted on the principle of reciprocity—that is, members of the research team also answered questions, provided information that members wanted, and responded to any requests for help with action on a pressing need for an individual or a family (Maiter, Simich, Jacobson, & Wise, 2008).

To facilitate effective sharing and exchange of information, the dialogues were conducted in Urdu and Farsi, the spoken languages in the two neighbourhoods. This is in keeping with what Fitzgerald (2004) suggested as a way of conducting research in cross-cultural contexts. The research team members who could communicate in the preferred language of the neighbourhood served as discussion facilitators. In addition, community volunteers acted as translators for those who spoke other languages.

In total, 143 older adults (75 women and 68 men) from both neighbourhoods participated in the dialogues over a three-month period. Even after the data collection had been completed, the agency continued its work in both communities through weekly drop-ins. The agency's continued involvement helped older adults enhance their leadership skills and strengthen their commitment to work on their issues.

New community leaders joined the existing research team and became actively involved in the data analysis and knowledge mobilization. The data analysis process began with the research team translating and organizing the findings into themes (Creswell, 2013). After the findings had been presented to and approved by the older adults and the RAC members, a discussion of knowledge mobilization strategies was launched. A number of my observations shaped the knowledge mobilization strategies. I presented these observations for discussion and validation during debriefing meetings with the research team.

First, similar to Freire's (2000) and Shulman's (1992) perspectives, there was a lot of shame and guilt among the older adults about their poverty, and they often held themselves responsible for the situations in which they found themselves. Second, I observed that the older adults in one of the neighbourhoods had little interaction with other community members. It seemed as though the older adults' shame about their living conditions had confined them to live in isolation. This was not the case with older adults living in the second neighbourhood. Third, despite their identity as South Asians, the majority of the older adults in both communities came from two countries of origin. During the last two decades, those countries have experienced strained political relations, and the tensions had influenced relations between the communities in Toronto. Each neighbourhood felt national pride for their country of origin and heritage, and simultaneously felt prejudice, a lack of trust, and a reluctance to work with the other community on any issue. While members of both neighbourhoods followed the same religion, the communities were extremely diverse. Each community, for example, had its own language and views about life for older adults (Buchignani, 2010). Older adults in the first neighbourhood, for example, limited themselves to religious prayers and some regional television programming; any other type of social entertainment was looked down upon by other community members. In contrast, older adults from the other neighbourhood had informal networks and conducted social activities from time to time.

These observations had significant implications in terms of the nature and design of the knowledge mobilization strategy. I realized that knowledge mobilization in this context needed to go beyond taking action on research findings. Most importantly, the knowledge mobilization strategy had to be transformative for community members. It also had to challenge the older adults' shame and guilt by connecting their personal plight to structural factors. Doing so would enable the older adults to feel motivated to take action. To accomplish this goal, I felt that special events needed to be planned in the communities. In order to draw a large number of community members, the events would have to be held in close proximity to the neighbourhoods, be culturally appropriate, and feature enjoyable social activities. I felt that the presence of a large number of community members at the events would likely create pressure on the area's city councillor and the local member of provincial parliament (MPP) to take action on the research findings. Given this scenario, I felt that the most suitable strategy of knowledge mobilization would be to use critical art forms that are grounded in cultural traditions of both communities, which had the potential to unsettle the status quo and initiate dialogue and action. I shared these reflections and discussed the various art forms with the rest of the research team, who also saw value in using an arts-based knowledge mobilization strategy. The research team decided to deliberate on suitable art forms with some older adult members in both communities.

After much discussion, the first neighbourhood decided to perform a play. For many community members, theatre has been used predominantly as a form of protest and resistance against political, religious, and gender-based oppression in their country of origin (Sengupta, 2014). Therefore, it was fitting to use a theatrical performance to draw attention to the social conditions of older adults in Canada, a technique proposed by Freire (2000) and O'Donoghue (2009). First, a script had to be developed for the play. To provide an accurate representation of the older adults' social realities, the play was based on the major findings and real-life narratives that had been obtained during the community dialogues.

The play was written and directed by an agency staff person who was also a member of the community, as well as an activist and a professional artist. In this manner, the play was a collaborative effort; the research team shared data with the staff member, who in turn shared his professional expertise. This strategy is suggested by Eisner (2008) to maintain the quality of the art. Care was taken to develop the script in Urdu, the preferred language of the community, so as to facilitate members' engagement with the performance and the issues it explored. According to Eastham and colleagues (2010), such engagement is critical for accomplishing social justice transformation. To that end, through a search in the community, the research team identified people who were committed to the issues and were interested in performing on stage, but also had no acting experience. Those community members were chosen to help the audience identify with the characters and the issues. The play focused on older adults' challenges and the need to take action to effect change. A pre-performance announcement explained that the script was based on actual research data. The audience was then asked to observe a moment of silence to recognize the older adults who had succumbed to the challenges they had faced while living in Canada. Lighting, sound effects, and translations were provided by community volunteers. A local photographer and a caterer were also hired to provide their services at the function. The play was staged at a community auditorium located in close proximity to the neighbourhood and was attended by 350 people, including community members, staff from community partner agencies, members from the funding agency, and the city councillor and the local MPP. A few people from the second research neighbourhood were also in attendance.

The second neighbourhood opted to use *mushaira*, a poetry recital, as a knowledge mobilization strategy. Mushaira is popular among older adults in the community. The mushaira was to focus on the themes that emerged from the research findings on the life of older adults from the local community in Toronto. An open invitation was sent to all older women and men from the community to present their poetry in Urdu and Farsi, the two predominant languages of the neighbourhood. In keeping with the principle of supporting local organizations, the function was held at a locally owned restaurant located in the neighbourhood. The function was attended by 200 people, including community members of all ages. Members of the other neighbourhood also attended with their religious leader. All guests were served culturally appropriate food. Since there were not enough seats to accommodate everyone, younger members in the audience stood through the program. The event provided local poets with the opportunity to present their perspectives and obtain recognition. The recital was well-received by the community. In fact, audience members and the restaurant owner felt the recital should continue beyond its original time allotment.

After the community events were held, the research team and the RAC reflected on the activities, and it was determined that the events had made an extremely positive impact among community members and stakeholders. The team, for example, received positive feedback from the stakeholders, and a joint action to address issues of food security was undertaken by the older adults along with community partner agencies and volunteers following the events. These outcomes are viewed as strong indicators of the success of the events. They also suggest that the use of critical art forms was beneficial as a knowledge mobilization strategy.

CRITICAL ARTS FOR EFFECTIVE KNOWLEDGE MOBILIZATION AND COMMUNITY ACTIVISM

Davison and National Collaborating Centre for Determinants of Health (NCCDH; 2013) assert that the most promising models of knowledge mobilization are those "with principles and values reflective of equity and social justice" (p. 13). Similarly, Briggs and colleagues (2015) recommend a community-led process of evaluation that takes into consideration the four R's: "Reach, Relevance, Relationship and Results" (p. 2). In this section, I will discuss the ways in which the critical arts strategy met all those objectives.

Both the theatrical performance and the poetry reading attracted a large and diverse group of community members. Using art forms to attract the attention of diverse stakeholders to community issues has been recommended by Briggs and colleagues (2015) and Ranta-Tyrkko (2010). That said, each event brought people together around an important issue. In the opinion of Parada, Barnoff, Moffatt, and Homan (2011), this is a critical precondition for organizing and mobilizing community. As Lee (2011) suggests, the presence of community members in large numbers could be attributed to their interest in the art form as well as their identification with the issue.

Unlike other forms of knowledge mobilization, the play and the recital combined entertainment with social justice and a change agenda. As Clover and Stalker (2005) have argued, such performances make social change and activism feel less threatening. The message of collective action presented in the play served to inspire realistic hope that change is possible, which allowed community members to collectively seek ways to address their challenges and reaffirmed their political agency in the days following the events (Freire, 2000). In keeping with the arguments made by Clover and Stalker (2005) and Quinlan (2010) regarding the significance of performance for its audience, the inclusion and participation of the older adults established an instantaneous, dialogic connection between the performers and the audience. The older adults in the audience identified with the issues and the characters. This was evident in the feedback received from the audience and specifically from a community member who contacted a staff member immediately after the play, to let her know that "he felt that he was being heard for the first time [in Canada]." A community member at the poetry recital had tears of joy in his eyes, for he felt that his culture was recognized and accepted in this country. In this way, the performances gave voice to those on the margins, who had lost their voice, and turned their personal narratives of suffering into a public issue. This was a critical step in politicizing the issue. This is very much in keeping with Gray's (2007) work around making the voices of marginalized women heard through research.

The performances also affected people from other generations. As Finley (2011) asserts, the other generations in the audience felt empathy for the older adults and were moved by them to take action. To that end, the performances led to increased interest among youth and adults to volunteer and support older adults. New relationships were formed among different age groups within the communities and also between members of both communities. Additionally, when individuals from one community attended the art performance in another community, new connections were forged and a new spirit of collaboration resulted. The same is also true of the community partner agencies. Many of them were moved to tap into their own networks and resources in order to address older adults' challenges. As recommended by ACT for CFS (2014), these developments not only strengthened the relationships among the communities and various stakeholders, but also led to new discussions and partnerships. Indeed, those efforts resulted in various community-wide actions to support older adults. This is in keeping with Levin's (2008) argument for an effective knowledge mobilization strategy. While these actions addressed the immediate and concrete material issues faced by older adults, they also brought about foundational changes in the life of these communities.

CONCLUDING THOUGHTS: CHALLENGES WITH ARTS BASED KNOWLEDGE MOBILIZATION

Although the research achieved many successes for the communities, there were several issues that had to be addressed throughout the KM process. They included debating the intent of dissemination events, using original narratives, and procuring funding to support the artists' training. The play, for example, involved a unique collaboration between the researchers and the professional artist—a collaboration that Eisner (2008) strongly supports. Even still, the partnership posed some challenges. A balance had to be struck between seeing the play as an end in itself and seeing it as a means to an end. The director saw the performance as a way to disseminate the research findings, therefore the quality of the performance was of paramount importance. I, on the other hand, viewed the play as a tool to spur the communities to take action. Therefore, in my opinion, the quality of the performance was not especially important. Some scholars have supported the former viewpoint while others have supported the latter (see Finley, 2011, for a fuller discussion). In the end, I agreed to prioritize the quality of the play. Ultimately, as Saladaña (2008) asserts, if the performance had not achieved a certain standard of excellence, it would not have been taken seriously by stakeholders and would have lost its impact.

The handling of the research data posed another challenge during the production of the play. The community artists wanted to make the script more captivating for the audience by altering the original narratives. I, however, had some concerns about this plan. The play was a performance of actual data, and as such, the authenticity of the data had to be retained. Modifying the narratives would have affected the process of having one's voice heard. The richness of the original narratives, and the contradictions within those stories, enabled audience members to identify with the characters and stories and thereby mobilize the research-generated knowledge. The narratives might have lost this impact if they had been altered.

Securing funding for the project also proved to be a major challenge, especially in order to spread the campaign and mobilize older adults in other parts of the city and the Greater Toronto Area. To accomplish that goal, the social service agency would have incurred the cost of paying the artists and technical support volunteers. In fact, the research team dealt with an ethical dilemma throughout the knowledge mobilization process: while the team was benefitting from the talents of local community members, many of whom were struggling financially, no payment was provided in return.

The research team also faced a dilemma of whether the same play could be performed in other communities. Introducing the play to different neighbourhoods would have undermined the development process behind the production and would have compromised the values that drove the project (i.e., recognizing the importance of local context, and honouring communities' ways of knowing and sharing). Upon critical reflection, I realized a paradox was at work. Despite good intentions, activism, and a desire to introduce the play to more audiences, I would have actually participated in colonial ways of knowledge production by attempting to impose the research findings from one community on another (Chilisa, 2012; Smith, 2012).

This chapter discussed the use of critical arts as an effective strategy for knowledge mobilization and community activism. Using two performances as examples, I have demonstrated that the arts can have a tremendous impact on a variety of stakeholders, including community members. Of course, there are challenges associated with using the arts for knowledge mobilization. Employing art in this manner, however, makes research a meaningful endeavour for marginalized communities, activists, and researchers who are committed to equity, social justice, and change.

NOTE

1. I would like to thank Danika Syrja McNally (MSW) for her contributions as Research Assistant on the development of this chapter.

4 | The Use of Photography in Anti-Oppressive Research

Samantha Wehbi, Professor, School of Social Work, Ryerson University

Despite a growing critique of the positivist and "rational" modes of knowing and doing in social work, the profession continues to be dominated by an emphasis on text at the expense of evocative or expressive forms of communication such as visual imagery (Chambon, 2008; Walton, 2012). Social work scholars argue for the need to make a place for the visual in social work, noting its importance for educating more well-rounded future practitioners able to express and cope with the complexities of their practice experiences (Boehm, 2004; Huss, 2012; Phillips & Bellinger, 2010; Tower, 2000). Others contend that the integration of visual imagery within social work practice is indeed not a new phenomenon and provide historical bases for such collaboration (Huff, 1998; Marshall, Craun, & Theriot, 2009).

While there has been relatively little reliance on visual methods compared to text in social work, the field of visual research has a somewhat lengthy history, specifically within sociology and anthropology, with dominance of photography as the preferred medium (Emmison & Smith, 2000; Harper, 2004). Starting with the use of photography in the work of Jacob Riis and Lewis Hine to document social concerns such as child labour and immigrant experiences in support of a social reform agenda in the late 1800s and early 1900s, the value of photographs as objective documentary records of reality has been somewhat unquestioned in the social sciences (Prosser, 1998; Trachtenberg, 1977). Of particular relevance for social work is the example of Hine's work with reformist social workers such as Jane Addams and the Settlement House Movement.

Moreover, social work scholarship dealing with visual research has focused on the use of photovoice, a method relying on "giving research participants cameras so that they can take photographs" (Leavy, 2009, p. 230). This method can be used to express everyday lived realities and social issues and enhance community engagement. Moreover, photovoice has been used as an approach to challenge marginalization, hence its great relevance for anti-oppression approaches to social work; indeed, its origins can be traced back to campaigning on issues of homelessness (Purcell, 2007). Moreover, photovoice is premised on the notion of favouring participation to enhance empowerment and, as such, it has been used as a method with traditionally marginalized populations (Ohmer & Owens, 2013), which again is a concern for anti-oppression researchers.

However, what I propose in this chapter is the need to *move beyond* an overreliance on photovoice. It is beyond the scope of this paper to provide a critique of photovoice based on a critical discussion of issues of participation, voice, authority, and so on—for a critical discussion of some of these issues in terms of the uses of art in community engagement, see Bishop (2006a, 2006b), Kester (2004), and George (this volume). Instead, in this chapter, I propose that we enlarge our vision of the uses of visual imagery in anti-oppression social work research by considering the many potential uses of photography beyond photovoice.

As such, this chapter aims to provide a comprehensive and nuanced discussion of the uses of visual imagery, specifically photography, in anti-oppression social work research. There is a wealth of information and available studies that demonstrate the vast potential of using photography in social research. As social workers interested in enhancing our education, practice, and research, this field merits further examination (Chambon, 2008). In this chapter, I discuss the uses of photography in research methodology and provide an example of a study to concretely illustrate the ideas presented here, demonstrating how they can contribute to anti-oppression.

TOWARD A CRITICAL USE OF PHOTOGRAPHY IN RESEARCH

Since the early work that utilized photography to document reality in support of social reform, photography's uses in social research have become more diverse. Rose (2012) differentiates between visual cultural studies, which examine found images, and visual research methods, which rely on "images as ways of answering research questions, not by *examining* images—as do visual culture studies—but by *making* them" (p. 10, emphasis in original). However, a more comprehensive approach to understanding visual research methods is offered by other scholars. In their historical review of the development of visual research, Emmison and Smith (2000, p. 22) note four approaches to the use of visual material in the social sciences: (1) production and analysis of visual images by researchers, (2) analysis of existing images, (3) analysis of "practices of visualization," and (4) use of video-recording to analyze interactions. The first two approaches have relied heavily on photography and, to a lesser extent, film. A documentary photography approach has been included in both of these approaches: In the first approach, photographs are generated to document a particular reality; in the second, documentary photographs such as those in news media are used in social science analysis.

In addition to critiquing the heavy reliance on photography as visual data, which is of less relevance to the present chapter, Emmison and Smith (2000), as well as Harper (2004), highlight the problematic nature of unquestioningly assuming that photographs document an unmediated reality. Harper notes that the subjectivity of photographs arises from the technical and social constructions of images; technical aspects such as framing, use of lenses, and so on, dictate the type of image produced, as do the social locations of the photographer and subjects. In this sense, photographs are seen as social constructions, not as objective records of reality. Rose (2012) echoes this observation by calling for a "critical visual methodology," which understands images as visual forms of culturally and socially constructed differences: "Looking carefully at images, then, entails, among other things, thinking about how they offer very particular visions of social categories such as class, gender, race, sexuality, able-bodiedness, and so on" (p. 12). Moreover, the author notes that critical forms of visual methodology require a reflexivity on the part of the viewer to understand their role as an audience member and how they contribute to the construction of meaning of images. Wiesing (2010) notes that the sense of an image is derived partly from how it is perceived by viewers, and hence, the viewer plays a role in determining the meaning of images. Indeed, the concepts of reflexivity and constructed social differences are key in anti-oppression social work, and as such, "critical visual methodologies" relying on photography as suggested by Rose (2012) are of great value for our discussion.

Furthermore, the above-noted need to engage reflexively with images and to think critically about how they construct and reflect social differences troubles the assumed objectivity of photographs, which is also raised by Ball and Smith (1992) in their discussion of photography in the social sciences. The authors argue that seeing photographs as records of reality is problematic not only because of the issues of framing referred to earlier but also from a methodological point of view. When seen as mirrors of reality, photographs are under-analyzed and used to serve as no more than a memory aid for field research. Ball and Smith encourage researchers to reconsider photographs as more than memory aids and to see their potential for analysis in decoding the meanings they reflect about ideology and socio-political contexts. In social science research, photographs need to be examined with as much awareness and critical analysis of their mediated and representational nature. For example, photographs have been used for political purposes such as supporting a colonial agenda (Mirzoeff, 1999; Ranger, 2001), a discussion I return to later in this chapter, as it is of relevance to the research example I will discuss.

Both qualitative and quantitative approaches have been utilized in the collection and analysis of existing images (Ball & Smith, 1992; Emmison & Smith, 2000). Within quantitative approaches, content analysis has been used by researchers to investigate a phenomenon under study at a particular point in time or to examine changes over time (Emmison & Smith, 2000; Walker & Chaplin, 1997). Content analysis is best described as a technique that "aims to establish the frequency with which certain categories or themes appear in the material investigated" (Ball & Smith, 1992, p. 21). For example, a classic study referred to frequently in the scholarship was undertaken by Richardson and Kroeber in 1940, wherein the researchers examined the changes in women's dress over a 330-year period, from 1605 to 1936, by looking at a variety of sources, including magazine photographs for more contemporary material (Ball & Smith, 1992; Emmison & Smith, 2000).

An important critique of the use of quantitative methods such as content analysis is the emphasis on the manifest content of photographs at the expense of an analysis of latent meanings (Ball & Smith, 1992). As Ball and Smith (1992) note, "frequency is a poor guide to the communicative significance or meaning of a particular item" (p. 28). In addition, in devising systems of categorization, a researcher breaks up an image, which may in fact be read in its totality—not as a set of characteristics. Furthermore, the classification system may have more to do with a researcher's theoretical framework or research paradigm than with how an image may be interpreted by others (Ball & Smith, 1992). Moreover, content analysis is claimed as an objective method of data collection and analysis due to its systematic "devising of precisely and clearly defined categories to apply" to the material being studied (Ball & Smith, 1992, p. 21). Claims of objectivity key in assessing the rigour of research within positivist frameworks have been heavily scrutinized within critical research paradigms (Leavy, 2009). Indeed, Prosser (1998) emphasizes that a theoretical framework is essential as a guide for the analysis of photographic data. Pink (2007) further emphasizes the importance of our underlying theories for understanding how the image-creation process, as well as the images themselves, construct knowledge.

In addition to relying on a theoretical framework, analysis of photographic images needs to be guided by considerations related to the actual images being analyzed, or what Rose (2012) refers to as the "site of the image" (p. 27), which includes technological and compositional elements. Framing, lighting, choice of equipment used to capture the image, and how the image is manipulated or handled by digital technologies are all examples of elements that need to be taken into account in analysis. Banks (2001) adds that when analyzing images, the actual content of images needs to be examined by looking at the internal and external narratives of the photograph. The internal narrative is understood as the meanings an image holds for its audience—as opposed to the meaning intended by the author of the image. These meanings are further enhanced and complicated by the external narrative of the image, which consists of the social context and social relations that surround the reading of the image. Fitzpatrick (2008) adds a layer of complexity to these questions by noting how images produced for a specific audience and purpose can have different meanings when placed in new frames, such as institutional publications. For example, the images taken by Del Tredici to critically document the atomic bomb and nuclear weapons production could be seen to communicate an anti-war message when first presented in 1987. The photographs were recirculated in 1993 within government publications about nuclear waste management. The accompanying text altered the meaning from when the images first appeared, de-emphasizing a critical message. Fitzpatrick's analysis highlights the importance of taking into account not only how and why images are first produced but also how they are open to reinterpretation depending on the new contexts within which they appear. In short, the analysis of images needs to take into account the image—what it looks like, how it is communicated to an audience, where it appears, and so on—and its contexts, as shaped by the photographer, the audience, and broader social relations.

RESEARCH EXAMPLE

For the purposes of the research example presented in this chapter, I rely on the second approach discussed by Emmison and Smith (2000), namely the analysis of existing commercially produced images. Specifically, I examine the images found in the public reports of Canadian international development agencies. This approach is most relevant considering the theoretical framework I chose for the research example; my study adopted an anti-oppression social work approach in conjunction with a postcolonial framework that highlights the continued power differentials in North/South relations. As part of a larger project (see Wehbi, 2010), this study sought to examine involvement in social justice efforts at the international level. Taking into consideration a key premise in visual culture studies that argues images are part of our everyday and not simply representations of it (Mirzoeff, 1999), analyzing existing images at once recognizes the pervasiveness of images, as well as their centrality in how we understand our world. As such, the photographs in international development reports are worthy of analysis because they could be seen not only to represent but also to inform and shape our understanding of social intervention in the global South.

Inscribing itself within a critical social science research paradigm, the present study steers clear of claims of objectivity and instead attempts to arrive at an understanding of how the images presented in international development reports reflect and reproduce a constructed "reality" that we, the audience, are meant to take at face value. By challenging these normative constructions, this study aims to contribute to challenging the power relations that undergird them and allow for their perpetuation. Hence, in line with the study's anti-oppression approach, qualitative methods of data collection and analysis are more suitable than, for example, content analysis, and these are described in more detail below.

The example presented in this chapter is based on a study that examined the development reports or newsletters—if no reports were available—of 50 Canadian international development agencies in the period 2006–2009, with a majority of available reports in the latter part of that time range. In keeping with the study's focus on North/South power relations, I selected agencies that noted social justice as part of their vision or mission. Such agencies would presumably be aware of differential power dynamics. These organizations included a mix of faith-based and secular agencies as well as regional, national, and coalition initiatives; all were under the national umbrella of development agencies, Canadian Council for International Co-operation (CCIC).

Data collection involved selecting the reports, and cutting out, categorizing, and filing the images and any associated captions. Data collection yielded 1,147 images, mostly of people (1,085) and some of nature and objects—such as a plough or a well. The images of people were predominantly of children and women, while a much smaller number of images were of men.

As noted earlier, a theoretical framework is a key guide in the analysis of data, including images. The anti-oppression approach to social work guiding this study allowed the research to begin from the premise of socially constructed differences that need to be challenged. Moreover, engaging reflexively with the images meant moving beyond what appeared on the surface, to examining how they reflect meaning and how that meaning is reflective of social relations of power. However, moving to the level of North/South relations, the study was also guided by a postcolonial lens as it is of direct relevance for the chosen research topic. Specifically, the analysis of the external narrative of the photographs was guided by the concepts of colonialism, neocolonialism, and imperialism, as well as by an understanding of critiques of development and foreign aid (Bhabha, 2010; Heron, 2007; Hoogvelt, 2001; Kapoor, 2008, 2012; Said, 1978, 1993, 1997; Wehbi, 2010).

Adopting this critical perspective is important for social work if we are to avoid reproducing oppressive relations through our international professional practice. As Razack (2009), Sewpaul (2006, 2007), and Moosa-Mitha (2014) contend in their discussion of social work practice, it is important for our profession to take into account the history of unbalanced colonial relations between global South and North and to respond by challenging these relations of power. These efforts, they argue, need to extend to how we perceive of our role as social workers acting in the transnational arena beyond merely offering services, to thinking reflexively about how we can resist oppressive relations. Building on these arguments, I am proposing that this critical reflection on our role also implies the need to engage reflexively with images, specifically how their external narratives could reproduce colonial, neocolonial, or imperialist discourses.

As for the internal narrative of the images, I relied on semiotic analysis, the study of images as signs (Barthes, 1982; Sontag, 1982; Walker & Chaplin, 1997; Wiesing, 2010). Wiesing (2010) notes that images do not necessarily have to function as signs—or symbols. However, an image takes on a sense or meaning when it is read within an understanding of how and why it was produced. In his works on semiotic analysis in photography, Barthes (1982) notes that images and accompanying text must be read for their denotative and connotative content, the latter of which can be discerned through an understanding of the broader context, including power relations in society. Indeed, Walker and Chaplin (1997) propose that uncovering these power relations is a key task for critical researchers.

The semiotic analysis of the images in the selected reports proceeded in five steps, as described by Penn (2000). The first step, described earlier, involved the selection of images. The second step consisted of compiling a "denotational inventory" of the contents of the images, including their accompanying captions. Where no captions were included, the accompanying text was read to extract references to the images, if any. The third step consisted of examining the connotative meaning of the images. In order to conduct this level of analysis, the external narrative of the image was considered: historical and contemporary context of North/South relations, development practice, foreign aid, and so on. The fourth step consisted of checking whether all the denotational elements of the images had been covered in the connotative analysis. The final step involved structuring and presenting the findings. As noted earlier, findings demonstrated a majority of images of children and women, usually with development workers.

For the purposes of demonstrating the ideas discussed in this chapter, I present the analysis of one image. As Wiesing (2010) notes, the study of images can consist of the analysis of a single image or a group of images. Hence, even though the broader study included analysis of several images, for the purposes of this chapter, I focus on the analysis of one image selected because multiple variations of it appear in various international development organizational reports. The image is that of a white development worker or volunteer holding a Black infant or child. A celebrity take on the image can be seen in the controversial 2006 work of Vanessa Beecroft, "White Madonna with Twins," in which the white artist photographs herself seated, wearing a white robe, breastfeeding two Black infants in Sudan (the image is available at http://www.vanessabeecroft.com/frameset.html). A subdued and seemingly less controversial, yet, I would argue, similar image can be found in the November 2006 newsletter of the Victoria International Development Education Association (VIDEA), a non-profit organization focusing on raising awareness about development issues. The image shows a white female intern in her early twenties standing with a sleeping Black baby held in a sling pouch on her back. The intern is facing the camera and smiling, while the baby's face is turned to the side. The image appears as part of an article on the experiences of the intern in Zambia. The caption identifies the intern by name and the geographical area—Lusaka—but does not make mention of the infant. The background of the image is a rural scene with local people seen in the distance.

The image contains several signs such as "Black child," "white woman," and "rural landscape." Each of these denotative elements carries its own connotations and acts as a metaphor that can be interpreted following a theoretical framework that takes colonialism into account. The Black child or, indeed, Africa as a helpless child in need of protection and civilization is not a new metaphor but one steeped in a history of colonial violence and white supremacy (Razack, 2004). The white woman, a symbol of purity and the moral superiority of Western civilizations, is upheld as an ideal to be attained and as a protector of "lesser" races, a carrier of burdens (Heron, 2007). The rural landscape has long functioned in photography as evidence of backwardness and traditionalism (Burns, 2004) that can only be remedied with the intervention of colonial saviours, in this case, international development agencies. In fact, the text accompanying the image is rife with reference to workshops and training conducted by the intern to teach the locals about human rights (for an analysis of the neocolonial discourses embedded in these reports, see Wehbi, 2010).

As for the formal elements of the image—the natural lighting used; the image is shot outdoors and shadows are apparent; the seemingly spontaneous posing of the subjects, as the woman is standing but turning as if in mid-stride and the baby is sleeping; as well as the seemingly un-posed and unfocused background—all convey a sense of naturalness in the image. The idea that photographs represent an unmediated reality is further accentuated by the "snapshot" feel of the image. In other words, the image signals that it is telling the "truth" about relations between white Canadians and Black Africans, or, more broadly, about the development relationship between North and South.

Moreover, to better understand the sense of the image, it must be placed in its dual contexts: the context of promotional material by international development agencies, and the context of development issues in Western societies such as Canada. Hence, while I present the analysis of this one image, it needs to be read as one example of a broader phenomenon—a similar image of a white woman holding the hand of a Black baby can be seen on the website of VIDEA (http://www.videa.ca/). Moreover, the newsletters and reports serve a marketing purpose, and in this sense they are akin to advertisements, full of symbolism that reflects and draws upon societal conventions shaped by discourses about the relationship between North and South. Put differently, the reports, sent to funders, volunteers, supporters, potential members, and others, are cultural artifacts that carry social messages (Hodder, 2000). When considered from a postcolonial framework, these messages about Northern benevolence and Southern helplessness and the need for development become apparent in the iconic image of the white woman caring for the Black child.

CONCLUSION

This chapter sought to examine the potential uses of photography in anti-oppression research. Following a survey of the methodological scholarship, I presented an example of a study that I conducted, adopting photo analysis as a method. My example presented the analysis of an image taken from a broader study that I conducted on international development. Through a lens focusing on colonialism, I engaged in semiotic analysis of the image and attempted to show some of its embedded discourses about North/South relations. While my example relies on photo analysis, my hope with this chapter is to encourage a consideration of photography in social work research. If the old adage that a picture speaks a thousand words holds any relevance, then photographs can indeed be used as tools to better understand our world in its complexities.

Section II

Unfolding Anti-Oppressive Research in Organizations

5 | Process as Labour

Struggles for Anti-Oppressive/ Anti-Racist Change in a Feminist Organization[1]

Ken Moffatt, Professor, School of Social Work, Ryerson University

Lisa Barnoff, Associate Professor, School of Social Work, and Dean, Faculty of Community Services, Ryerson University

Purnima George, Associate Professor, School of Social Work, Ryerson University

Bree Coleman, Field Education Coordinator, School of Social Work, Ryerson University

ANTI-OPPRESSION ORGANIZATIONAL CHANGE AND DEVELOPMENT

Anti-oppression is a model that has become prevalent in social work practice, which is rooted in earlier radical, anti-racist, feminist, and structural social work traditions (Campbell, 2003; Dominelli, 2002a). Promoting equity, inclusion, transformation, and social justice as fundamental aspects of social work practice, this approach aims to eliminate the multiple, interlocking manifestations of oppression, both within and beyond social work practice (Campbell, 2003; Dominelli, 2002b; Mullaly, 2002). Anti-oppression practice is not limited to one level of practice, as all levels are understood as interconnected and as being necessarily sites of struggle and change (Dominelli, 2002a). The goals of anti-oppressive work are twofold: to provide practical, frontline assistance to those who are injured by the oppressive social order and to engage in diverse efforts that are aimed at change that will transform oppressive systems (Dominelli, 2002a). Thus, an anti-oppression approach integrates the realms of micro- and macro-practice, recognizing the interactions between the personal and the political (Fook, 1993; Spratt, 2005).

All levels of social work, including theory, practice, research, and education, are being reconsidered from the anti-oppressive perspective (Wilson & Beresford, 2000). When the anti-oppressive literature has focused on practice, it has tended to emphasize social work education or clinical practice (Karabanow, 2004; Heron, 2004).

Nevertheless, the difficulty of introducing anti-oppressive approaches in practice has been exacerbated by the lack of literature related to integrating antioppression practice at the organizational level. We contribute to a better understanding of how social service agencies need to change to positively support anti-oppressive organizational work.

When considering the topic of organizational change, it is important to understand the distinction between the discrete philosophies of "managing diversity" and "anti-oppressive organizational change" (Barnoff, 2002). While the former is based predominantly on facilitating attitudinal and behavioural change within service providers in order to work more effectively with cultural "others," the latter is focused on creating change in the fundamental structures of power and privilege within organizations (Barnoff, Parada, & Grassau, 2004). A number of authors have begun to explore issues of identity within the field of anti-oppressive organizational practice (see, for example, Baines, 2002; Barnoff, 2001; Barnoff & Moffatt, 2007; Dominelli, 2002b; Gutierrez & Lewis, 1999; Hyde, 2004; Karabanow, 2004).

A widespread consensus exists among authors that the elimination of one form of oppression necessarily requires efforts to eradicate all forms (Baines, 2000; Dei, 1999; Ward, 2004), although most acknowledge the difficulty of addressing multiple oppressions (McLean, 2003). Baines (2007), Barnoff (2001, 2002), and Barnoff and Moffatt (2007) have begun to look at anti-oppressive organizational structures that address multiple, interlocking oppressions. Within such organizations, an anti-oppression agenda, including a focus on power relations, is integrated throughout all organizational systems, structures, and processes, and anti-oppression is viewed as a responsibility shared by all organizational members (Barnoff, 2001).

At the same time, some authors argue that an anti-oppression model, which attempts to focus on all oppressions simultaneously, can render specific forms of oppression invisible. As a result, some suggest that a single oppression lens should be maintained in order to be effective in terms of social change. Schiele (2007), for example, argues that the ascendency of anti-oppression, which treats all oppressions as equal, diminishes the focus on matters of race. The call for anti-oppressive approaches is too easily equated with an "equality of oppression" paradigm so that the pervasiveness and persistence of racism is not adequately addressed. Barnoff and Moffatt (2007) highlight how a similar concern exists for many frontline feminist practitioners; that is, that the focus on the intersectionality of oppression will diminish the focus on anti-racist practices.

Issues of participation and representation have been common in the literature of anti-oppression organizational change, aimed at allowing people who have been traditionally disenfranchised to have voice and power to affect organizational outcomes (see, for example, Barnoff, 2001; Guberman, Lamoureux, Fournier, Beeman, & Gervais, 2003). San Martin and Barnoff (2004), however, critique organizational change models that promote "inclusion" on only a superficial level. Such inclusion tends to revolve around hiring token women of colour and offering cultural food and celebrations, but avoids the critical issue of unequal power distribution that gives privilege to white women.

Feminist agencies represent one sector that has been identified as being at the forefront of integrating anti-oppression approaches into their organizational systems by directly facing the difficult controversies and challenges associated with social change (Baines, 2002). These challenges include internal agency issues, such as political contention and power struggles between women with different social identities, most visibly between women of colour and white women (Barnoff & Moffatt, 2007; Huygens, 2001; San Martin & Barnoff, 2004; Wilson, 1996). Barnoff (2001) remarked on the challenge to "move beyond words" and take concrete actions to eradicate oppressions, because only such actions will build trust with groups of women who have historically been marginalized in feminist organizations. Barnoff and Moffatt (2007) argue that the feelings of ongoing exclusion based on a particular social location when an organization attempts to deal with oppression by addressing intersectionality should be taken seriously in order to address change. Organizational leaders are essential to the process of facilitating organizational commitment and to the overall process of guiding organizational change (Barnoff, Parada, & Grassau, 2004).

Feminist organizations have historically seen patterns of outright resistance to anti-racist change from white women (Barnoff, 2002; Robertson, 1999; Wilson, 1996). Srivastava's (2005) and Srivastava and Francis's (2006) work focuses on the social relations of emotion in the anti-racist practice of feminist organizations. Srivastava (2005) finds that emotions are a prominent feature in anti-racist organizational struggles. In particular, two emotional patterns based on racial identity are drawn upon and perpetuated in these struggles—"angry woman of colour" and "tearful white woman." Srivastava argues that the emotional responses of white women to anti-racist challenges brought forth by women of colour often derail efforts to implement anti-racist organizational change.

At the same time that there has been an increased interest in anti-oppression models of delivery of practice, the socio-political environment has made the implementation of these changes difficult to accomplish. Due to the increasing withdrawal of resources for social services, service delivery has been simplified so that a narrower range of issues and needs facing service users are being addressed (Aronson & Sammon, 2000). The forced abandonment of politically conscious, preventative practice in favour of tightly regulated residual assistance has become a major challenge confronting social services (Aronson & Sammon, 2000). The current practice, characterized by economic efficiency, managerialism, and technocratic approaches, has been a response to pressures of globalization (Healy, 2000). These outcomes are making it difficult for non-governmental organizations to maintain a progressive practice that is committed to social justice and social change (Barnoff, George, & Coleman, 2006).

There is little scholarly work that documents the importance of process in developing anti-oppressive organizational structures. Further, it is important to examine agencies that have moved beyond basic attempts at diversity, such as hiring a diverse staff and engaging in regular training, and are now involved in more integrated approaches to implementing anti-oppressive organizational practices. We document some of the struggles that exist among women who are deeply committed to anti-oppressive organizational change within a feminist organization. We illustrate how, in spite of being situated in an organization that is structured on principles of anti-oppression, has done many years of work in this area, and has been identified as one of the "successes" in terms of anti-oppression organizational change, and in spite of the best honest intentions of its members, struggles persist in terms of the implementation of anti-oppression and anti-racist practices.

THE RESEARCH

The following analysis is based upon a case study of this feminist agency. We became interested in the agency that is the focus of this study since the members of this agency illustrate a historical commitment to anti-oppressive approaches. This feminist agency has made a concerted attempt to ensure anti-oppression manifests throughout the entire working environment of the agency. This particular agency has a reputation within the feminist social service community as one of the leaders in implementing anti-oppression practices.

We studied the organization in depth by interviewing all staff members, who covered every function within the agency. Due to the conscious effort of the agency members to reflect the diverse communities within which the agency is located, the interviewees are also diverse according to race and sexuality. The self-identified races of the interviewees included two Latin Americans, one First Nations, one Jewish Israeli, one white, and two who did not identify their race. All of the interviewees were women. The focus of this chapter was derived by working inductively from interview data to develop themes and new knowledge about major areas of transformative work. The researchers considered the most important themes through repetition in the interviews, relevance to the literature, and then grouped the themes by their interrelationship to each other.

The organization is a sexual assault centre with a long history in the feminist service sector. The staff provide sexual violence support services, including individual and group counselling. The mandate of the organization has expanded in response to the needs of diverse communities so that it now includes community outreach and services extending beyond its original mandate of counselling. It is a small organization with seven full-time staff members and a large group of part-time staff. The director makes clear that the agency's commitment and process defined by anti-oppressive approaches has a long history. The agency has been involved in a 15-year-long process with a commitment to equity, equality, and diversity. A full-time, permanent staff position has been devoted to diverse communities for the past ten years. This person's role is to provide specific specialized services within the community to deal with the fact that the organization historically had been a mostly white, mainstream feminist organization.

Over the years, the work of organizational members on issues of equity and equality has been manifest through various plans and strategies such as an equity action plan, an anti-racism plan, and, currently, a review with respect to anti-oppression. As the director of the organization states, these "formal plans and processes [are from] many, many years ago"; she reminds us that "it's not new work" in the agency. Currently, the organization describes its practice as being framed by an "anti-racist/anti-oppression" lens. It uses this terminology as a way of recognizing that not all forms of oppression are similar, and to ensure that its past focus on anti-racism does not get lost under the new umbrella of "anti-oppression."

The critique of feminist thought for its overreliance on white, Eurocentric thought, upon which the organization was based, led to change beginning in the late 1980s. At the same time, the organization has had to respond to community needs and criticisms due to its urban location among a number of diverse communities. When the director was hired, a key expectation of the hiring was that she put into practice a commitment to anti-racism/anti-oppression work and that she have an understanding of what kinds of organizational processes that commitment might result in. The director explains, "I am not an anti-racism/anti-oppression expert. It is just [that] I had to demonstrate that I had some commitment, and willingness to move on it, in leadership." As she states, her leadership needs to balance historical change and commitments with defining new directions for the organization: "I was to take the [anti-oppression] work that's happened [up to now] and try to do some new things with it. Not new things, continuation, [to] take it to another place as well."

To strengthen this historical commitment to anti-oppression and anti-racism, the members of the organization have made a recent choice to become involved in a process of evaluating the organizational commitment to social justice and how that commitment impacts practices and structures within the organization. This reflects a conscious choice of agency staff to become engaged more fully in anti-racist and anti-oppression work. An external consultant was hired to engage staff in a process of review. The consultant helped the staff reconsider the strategic plan and engaged in a series of meetings with all agency staff.

FINDINGS: STRUGGLES TOWARD ORGANIZATIONAL CHANGE

Throughout our interactions with staff and the analysis of interviews, we discovered that organizational members need processes to understand the struggles associated with change. In spite of the progressive nature of the organization and the visionary focus of its members, struggles persist. Based on our analysis, we are able to outline some specific ways in which struggles within the organization are manifest.

In spite of this long history of process and commitment to anti-oppression, there has been a parallel process of resistance in the form of struggles toward change within the organization. As one participant explained, "we had to stop being self-congratulating about how great we are, and look at how ugly and bad things still are and look at who was walking and not walking through our doors. ... There had to be a process of learning how to start [the organizational change work] again ... a process of ass-kicking." She explains anti-racism/anti-oppression work is like "levels of an onion, you go and you peel the next layer and then you can stop for five minutes and be happy you're there, but then you have to go [at it] again."

A worker describes a similar constant rethinking of anti-oppression process when she explains, "We had diverse communities meeting here, clusters of women coming, [but the] status quo is the same. It was kind of change for a while, but then it still keeps the same." In addition, the need to build in a structural mechanism to ensure an ongoing process of organizational change work that is filled with tensions and struggles—that are often felt in a deeply personal manner—resulted in the formation of an "anti-racism/anti-oppression committee" in this agency.

The struggle has not resulted in a lagging commitment among members but rather a lag in practice that illustrates their commitment—a lag in "how we do things." According to a staff member, the resistance to or struggles with anti-racism and anti-oppression work are subtle. It manifests as "that is not the way work is done in our organization" or in the idea that the work has no historical precedent:

> It was all really subtle. I am not talking about resistance in the way that people would ever articulate. But I think [the consultant] has come to help us see how those practices we had were forms of resistance [to anti-racism/anti-oppression change]. And the way we did not support certain programs and didn't work together were forms of resistance ... you know ... "we can't do that because that won't work" or "we've never done that that way before." Fear of change, that was resistance. When I say resistance, I'm talking about that real subtle ... bad, horrible kind of resistance that's really hard to sort of snip out.

At times, it is difficult to deal with the struggle because what is being resisted is not clearly articulated in a direct fashion, and often not even known to the person who is engaging in the struggle. Struggle over change is manifest as an argument for current practices; the importance of supporting the culture of the organization and the status quo; and the efficacy of practice.

Personal Emotions as Struggle

Struggles within the organization have been manifest as personally felt reactions to change. A participant explains that part of the process of developing an anti-racism/ anti-oppression perspective within the organization has involved:

> huge resistance from women, like personal resistance, to all the sort of inclusion work. That was when we had first begun that process, of trying to become more inclusive ... and [with] anti-oppression/anti-racism work, there is going to be resistance. We know that now. We did not know it then [when we started this work]. Because it wasn't like there was a manual you could take off the shelf that said, "okay, you want to do AR/ AO work ... here are the things to expect." Like now when I train volunteers, part of what I say to them up front in doing AR/AO work is, "there's going to be resistance. It's okay." And so we talk about it. But we didn't even know what it was back then, but we knew some feelings were coming up, but we sort of plowed ahead [anyway].

The struggle is manifest through a variety of emotions including fear. This organizational member goes on to explain that at the beginning of the organization's struggle to implement anti-racist practices,

> [It] was all so personal back then. Right? It was all so personal ... I think that there needs to be a support system in place to allow women the opportunity to express those things ... [like] the fear. I remember clearly, the fear for me as a white woman, I didn't want to express anything because I would be called racist. And there was incredible fear around that, and there was lots of fear of being attacked ... and that was one of our pitfalls. We didn't give ourselves permission. We weren't patient. We weren't patient. We didn't know what resistance was. We didn't know. I mean it was huge, in my opinion.

Another worker agrees about the personal nature of struggle when she states,

> Different ideas and resistance to change, the internal resistance [is important]. Because sometimes people say, "oh, I am not racist and I believe in equality" but the resistance is inside, you know? It's not outside. And we see that is still in some people here that are still working with us. They want change ... but ... it's like when we said we need to unlearn the power and control, we need to unlearn the racism and we are not doing that because it is rooted and it's hard. But they're here and we need to do the changes.

In this manner, the multi-layered quality of anti-oppression is manifest. Concepts such as psychological emotional structure versus environmental change need to be rethought. Anti-oppression work involves the emotional psyche as well as the social structures since they are interlinked. Based upon an increasing awareness among organizational members about the realities of these personal forms of resistance, or struggle, the organization has embarked on a process to begin identifying and then sharing what personal resistance looks like for each of them. Collective members discuss how resistance is manifest and how struggle is felt emotionally. Agency members talked with us about the flip-chart paper that is hanging on the wall from their last planning meeting; on this chart is the work of beginning to document this struggle. This exercise of making visible the forms of their personal resistance allows organizational members to challenge each other when they see or hear these forms of resistance in interactions within the agency.

Professionalism as a Form of Struggle

Resistance to change is also manifest in the professional stature of staff members who base their interventions on technical, professional posturing and knowledge. One worker discussed how the professionalized practice of a "neutral" counsellor who does not interact with service users in a manner that seems authentic, or the counsellor who does not show her feelings, is problematic when one views practice from an anti-racism/anti-oppression lens.

> R: Once what happen[ed], a woman took some pills, she wanted to die. And she went to the hospital. When I came to the shelter, the other [staff] told me, "there is a woman in the hospital because she took so many pills and she may come back tonight." So she came [back] … and she started to [scream]. [I asked] "What happened?" [She said] "Oh, I feel cramps in my legs!" The other [staff] was Canadian and she was panicking. I know from my country that when you have cramps, you [do] massage so that will help. So I said to her, "Do you want me to massage?" [She said] "Please, do whatever!" So I start to massage her and the [other] worker came [and said] "What are you doing?!" She yell[ed] at me. "Don't touch her!" I continued because she was telling me, "I feel good, thank you very much." So [the other worker] ran to call the hospital and they offered to her, [it is OK to] give her a massage. "OK," she says, "OK, you can do that." So the woman was so appreciative, and then she start[ed] to talk to me. And we were talking, and at the end it was like 4:00 in the morning. And she said, "well now I am going to bed." And I ask[ed] her, "Can I give you a hug?" She went, "Please." And I keep care of her. And it was [after] then, [that] she wanted a hug every day. [She] said, "Nobody hug me, ever."

> I: And you brought that kind of wisdom here?

R: And I said to the [other staff here] "You know, women sometimes need that. It's not always that we are going to [go around constantly] hugging women. But women need that. Women need to see in our faces that we are sorry for their pain, you know, with what is happening with them." So things were changing, you know, [the other staff said] "OK, maybe we can talk about that." So we went to find research studies that said that [touching] is all right. [laughs] And it's funny, you know, everything has to be scientific here. … You know, [my feminism] is from experience, it's from the praxis that we have in our own countries, you know. All the women struggle a lot, you know, against injustice and against all the things that is happening in our countries. And here, they have everything.

Through her recounting of this story, this staff member was able to illustrate to us some of the ways in which "professional" practices—dominant practices—are problematic to women from communities that have been marginalized. When working to integrate anti-oppression practices, agencies need to pay careful attention to the context of practice—to how dominant cultural norms and social realities facing women influence the forms that practice takes. In these instances, struggle emerges when agency members are not willing to explore the ways in which their current "neutral," professional practices might be based on a particular social reality, which could potentially be exclusionary for groups of women.

Struggle with Programming

At the organizational level, struggle with change manifested in the creation of a single program that has primary responsibility for promoting the agency's anti-racism/anti-oppression work. The agency is now struggling to work on this issue, to learn how best to integrate a focus on anti-racism/anti-oppression in all organizational programs:

Yeah, and I think the expectation that all programs have to integrate AR/AO practice [is important]. Whereas I think theoretically that was supposed to be happening, it really fell on that [one] program [to do the bulk of the AR/AO work]. So we were doing that classic thing of having this marginalized program, you know, which you're never supposed to do. And why I'm still so committed to having that program is because of how it's functioning now, and that it doesn't feel marginalized, and so I hope that it doesn't feel marginalizing. [We now know that] programs should integrate. So there became much more expectations around, what is your program doing to address the needs of women from diverse communities [rather than just relying on the one program to do all the work].

Organization members told us that the type of service traditionally offered in feminist sexual assault centres, based on a Western notion of one-to-one counselling, creates an organizational barrier to change:

> One of our educators, she's a woman who's originally from [an overseas region]. She says, "we have to start a dancing group. Because women in this community need to come together and dance." And "can we get some space here?" ... But I have to do some mental gymnastics around, "how can I spin that for a funder?" I immediately get why it would be very important—that women heal in different ways and that a particular model of healing, which is me and you sitting down in a room and, either individually or in a group, talking about sexual violence is a model, it's not the model. And I can get how a group of women from that community dancing together who have all experienced like massive rape as a part of war, or cultural genocide or ... I get that, but it's like, OK, how am I going to help people get that, or how am I going to find money for that ... to help funders get that? ... Because I think it's about exploring different modalities of healing, which is not usually done. So again, it's that thing that [the consultant] kept saying to us, "your organization should look absolutely different if you're doing AR/AO work. The kinds of things you do, the way you do them, should look different if you're doing it. If it doesn't, then you're not doing it."

The trouble with separate initiatives that represent immigrant women through "add-on" groups for diverse communities is that they became a form of tokenism.

> We had diverse communities [of women] meeting here but the status quo was the same. It was kind of a change for a while, but then it still again kept the same. The women came, [but] we had this problem, and this is our token. [Some people felt] "now we are more inclusive what you are talking about? We [do] have clusters [of diverse groups of women] here." But yeah, the clusters were there and nothing [else] was happening. Women were coming and going, but nothing was happening because at that time we had [only] two white counsellors, very white counsellors. [laughs]

Even when diversity had been built into some functions of the agency, the core funded practice of the organization—that is, one-to-one counselling—remained unchanged. This form of practice is not welcoming to all practitioners or potential clients. In effect, the agency had added on some forms of practice while not changing the fundamental nature of its work.

> So nothing was happening. And [diverse groups of] women weren't coming to the counselling, you know? And when I ... I had some women here from the Spanish

community, I had to go [with them to their counselling sessions at this agency] and be the translator for them. And what I saw, it was so cold. The counselling, it was so cold.

Acknowledging the difficulty in making anti-oppression change within an organization, the collective decided to create the anti-racism/anti-oppression committee and to make it compulsory to attend meetings. The purpose of the forum is to deal openly with the struggles associated with introducing change within the organization. In addition, the committee ensures that staff do not cope with struggle by simply withdrawing from the difficult work of making anti-racism/anti-oppression principles present in their practice. We see that, even in the most progressive organizations where consensus for change exists, there is a slippage of practice within the organizational structure. Furthermore, within one of the most innovative structures within this progressive agency, avoidance of struggle becomes present through education when what is required is attention to process.

CONCLUSION

The findings make clear the need to define process as an important form of labour that needs to be made visible within an organization undergoing anti-oppression organizational change. Furthermore, it reminds us that the work of anti-oppression is ongoing, always difficult, and "without end"; this open-ended, difficult process is what we have named as struggle within the organization. The term *struggle* is used to connote that the desire for change may exist while the means to achieve change is difficult. At times, even with best intentions, collective members resist the change they consider to be ideal. The work of process focused on anti-oppression is essential to the purpose of the organization, but is made invisible. Support for the work of process should be present in policy frameworks that guide both the organization and its funding bodies.

When one considers policy and practice, one has to anticipate the struggles associated with change. Even in progressive settings, literacy is required in human relations in order to promote anti-oppression change. In anticipation of struggles and resistance, all aspects of the agency need to be considered in order to implement change. Addressing oppression through specialized programs or hiring practices is inadequate so long as the organization does not also address its overall structure, mission and purpose, and engagement among organizational members.

The findings of this research indicate that the naming of the problem and the provision of guidelines is not adequate. Anti-oppressive organizational change and practices should be defined as open-ended and open to constant change and reconsideration. Policy that addresses anti-oppression would include statements about the dialectic nature of practice and principle, an integrative understanding of the nature of personal emotions and social change, and, most importantly, the best ways to define processes that are open to struggle rather than avoiding it.

Organizations committed to change need to build within their structure places for process where disagreements can occur, where troubling practices can be challenged, and where consensus can be reformulated among organizational members. Leadership of the organization needs to be comfortable with guiding members through contradictory processes and ambiguous relationships. Processes among organizational members, even though focused on a shared goal, may be confusing and tense.

The policy definition of professional work needs to be redefined so that practice most often associated as soft skills, such as those tied to relationship-building, cultural engagement, and awareness of processes of exclusion, are central to the definition of professional practices. The professional ability to develop a critical analysis of subjective engagement is likely more important than the neutral participation of professionals. Furthermore, political commitment to change grounds the professional so that she or he can challenge her- or himself in practice.

It is clear that the struggle of members to change the nature of their labour so that it is congruent with principles of anti-racism and anti-oppression is a concern shared by all. The women in this agency are deeply committed to working together and to continuing to develop organizational processes that deal with change toward a more just and equal form of service delivery, so much so that they are willing to engage in processes together that include emotional reactions based on deeply felt beliefs. This is the struggle we are discussing here, not a struggle defined too simply as a reaction against change but one that involves a commitment to work through very difficult and, at times, painful social processes. Attention to process is a fundamental aspect of how this agency operates to maintain its commitment to anti-oppression, and it is a valuable lesson to learn for all of us who are concerned with social justice–oriented social work practices.

NOTE

1. Reprinted and reformatted for this book with permission from Moffatt, K., Barnoff, L., George, P., & Coleman, B. (2009). Process as labour: Struggles for anti-oppressive/anti-racist change in a feminist organization. *Canadian Review of Social Policy, 62*, 34–54.

6 | Carrying Out Research on Whiteness, White Supremacy, and Racialization Processes in Social Service Agencies

June Ying Yee, Associate Professor, School of Social Work, Ryerson University

Processes of whiteness (Perry & Shotwell, 2009; Twine & Gallagher, 2007; Yee, 2005), white supremacy (Allen, 2001; Berg, 2012; Brown, 2009), and racialization (Galabuzi, Das Gupta, James, Roger, & Andersen, 2007; Martinot, 2003; Omi & Winant, 1986) are key concepts to be theoretically and empirically explored in critical scholarly research on whiteness. Early critical studies of whiteness focused mainly on ethnographic accounts and personal narratives (Allison, 2000; Bailey, 1999; Twine & Gallagher, 2007). According to Twine and Gallagher (2007), a "third wave" of research is emerging in the interdisciplinary area of whiteness studies, with an emphasis on critiquing Western institutional, state, and ideological belief systems that maintain white privilege through the deployment of whiteness strategies. Other scholars (Floyd, 2007; McDonald, 2009) have argued that there is now a "fourth wave" in race research, which aims to address "the limitations of essentializing race, advance arguments around the social construction and deconstruction of racial categories, re-examine race and racism within broader theoretical frameworks, and connect power, ideology and white hegemony, to illustrate how whiteness is perpetuated and internalized" (Arai & Kivel, 2009, p. 459). In other words, centring the analysis on race allows for a nuanced and detailed understanding of the ways in which the strategies and processes of whiteness hold power over the racialized "other."

At a practical and institutional level, rarely are connections made about the relationships between whiteness, white supremacy, and racialization processes in social service agencies' institutional practices. This is mainly due to the reality that everyday workplace institutional practices are generally considered to be fair, neutral, and value-free actions that are taken for granted as the way to do things (Henry & Tator, 2010; Yee & Dumbrill, 2016). Although qualitative research studies (Pon, Gosine, & Phillips, 2011; Yee, Wong, & Janczur, 2006) have documented people of colour's experiences of white racism in the workplace, more research is required to explore how these institutional practices are situated in a historical and globalized system of white supremacy. According to Allen (2001), "rather than seeing white supremacy as an outcome or sidebar to class relations, the critical race theory on the globalization of white supremacy radically and contingently places race at the center of analysis as it is the dividing line between white Leftists and most people of colour" (p. 468). Allen (2001) further argues that the "Marxist discourse on neoliberalism seems to pay little attention to naming explicitly and theorizing the racialization of neoliberalism and the continuing legacy of European imperialism" (p. 473).

The intent of this chapter is to explore, in practical terms, the often not discussed ways in which white supremacy undergirds social service agencies' institutional practices. Such an exploration is consistent with Moffatt, Barnoff, George, and Coleman's (this volume) argument that organizations need to move away from an emphasis on attitude and behavioural changes of those working in organizations to creating change in the power and privilege that resides within the structures of organizations. They have noted that even progressive (that is, feminist) organizations resist attempts at anti-racist organizational change. Given this reality, this chapter begins by defining whiteness and racialization and their relationship to white supremacy. Secondly, a historical account of the social work profession is given with details on the significant role that white women and the Christian church played in embedding white supremacist values in the method, system, and practices of the profession. Thirdly, the rationale for applying the concept of white supremacy in this research is discussed. Fourthly, I examine how a culture of white supremacy operates in the everyday workplace and provide a few recommendations on how to address it. I conclude by highlighting the importance of a racial analysis that integrates knowledge of white supremacy in research on white racism within social service agencies' institutional practices.

PROCESSES OF WHITENESS AND RACIALIZATION AND THEIR RELATIONSHIP TO WHITE SUPREMACY

Whiteness is a social and cultural process that confers power and privilege on those who are white. In other words, white people are racialized into a place of privilege. White people's power stems from the historical and present-day advantage they hold in determining and controlling the norms and values of Canada's social, political, and economic institutions. Coming from a place of whiteness can also apply beyond race. Whiteness may include coming from a place of structural advantage in terms of gender, class, sexual identity, and ability (Yee, 2005). Specifically, Gabriel (1998) argues that whiteness operates through three important mechanisms: (1) exnomination, (2) naturalization, and (3) universalization. Exnomination refers to the power that white people hold by virtue of making their racial status, that is, their whiteness, invisible to others. Naturalization is the ability of whiteness to always define who or what is non-white, but never itself. Not only do white people have the power to determine society's normative values, biases, and cultures based on their own socio-historical vantage point, but this power also grants them an unfair advantage in being able to shape, if not negate, the worldview of others. Finally, universalization is the power of white people to dominate the knowledge-making of all worldviews and ignore or diminish the validity of other life worldviews. To carry out acts of whiteness requires the racialization of the "other."

Processes of racialization occur when people interact with different systems and, due to their race, are afforded advantage or disadvantage. For example, white people hold structural advantages when accessing and/or participating within institutional systems that represent their norms and values and address their needs and aspirations. In contrast, people of colour are unfairly disadvantaged when the system attributes negative biases to their skin colour and they experience barriers within institutional systems. Therefore, processes of racialization rely upon the strategies of whiteness in order to maintain and justify this system of inequality. To be able to understand who benefits from the deployment of strategies and processes of whiteness requires an understanding of white supremacy.

The roots of white supremacy rest on the colonization and denigration of the worldviews of those who do not embody or adopt the European/Western worldview of civilization, progress, and science (Allen, 2001; Gordon, 1997; Thobani, 2007). Bery (2014) argues that if white supremacy is not named in any social or institutional process, then initiatives aimed at diversity such as multiculturalism can "reproduce dominant racial/racist ontologies, epistemologies and practices, albeit in new dis/guises" (p. 334). Both Bery (2014) and Seawright (2014) agree that the privileged epistemology that North American settler colonialists upheld is predicated on an "*ideal* white male settler actor" (Seawright, 2014, p. 554). This is why Seawright calls for settlers to epistemologically position themselves within structures and systems of power. Such awareness will reveal their place of domination and explain why those with epistemic privilege resist its own undoing.

Canada is a white settler society that was developed by European nations that colonized Aboriginal Peoples and their land to establish dominance, power, and control over Turtle Island (Baskin, 2011; McKenzie & Morrisette, 2003; Yee & Wagner, 2013). According to McKenzie and Morrissette (2003), "colonization is not simply a historical event; instead, its effects continue to obscure the world view of Aboriginal people and their related values and traditions" (p. 258). In fact, Lawrence and Dua (2005) critique anti-racism theory for not adequately addressing the oppression of Aboriginal Peoples. As a consequence, anti-racism theory itself is seen to be in need of decolonization. Likewise, the racialization of people of colour and their subordination and oppression cannot be addressed until white people deal with past and continuing forms of white supremacist values that undergird the practices, systems, and policies of Canada's institutions.

According to Allen (2001), white supremacy is a global phenomenon that relies upon five key features. The first is European imperialism, based on the notion of a superior white race, which offers a structure for white people to benefit from the exploitation of people of colour and their lands while simultaneously blaming people of colour for their own exclusion and, in turn, rationalizing this system of oppression as natural (Baldwin, 2012; Bery, 2014; Seawright, 2014). A powerful example of this is how legal institutions legitimized white people's racism against Black people by validating slavery in the modern era. Since the Enlightenment period, "others" who live in Africa, Asia, Australia, and the Americas have been historically perceived as "savage" and "uncivilized" by the "civilized" white race; this is the second feature (Kincheloe & Steinberg, 1998; Levine-Rasky, 2013; Yancy, 2007). The third feature is how nation-states in Africa and the Americas "were spatially developed by Europeans to drain the land of materials and 'Othered' bodies in order to feed the white flesh and white desires" (Allen, 2001, p. 480). This geopolitical system not only created a hierarchy unto the bodies of racialized "others," but also "enable[d] whites to have little trouble when it comes to blaming the indigenous and diasporic people of the world for their own victimization under global white supremacy" (p. 480). The fourth feature of global white supremacy is structurally manifested in local sites of interaction between white people and people of colour (Fiske, 1998; Gilroy, 1991; Smith, 2014); that is, "whites, whether knowingly or not, act as agents of whiteness in the surveillance of white territories, thus constructing psycho-social spaces of trauma and alienation, such as schools, for people of colour" (Allen, 2001, p. 480). The fifth feature is embedded in the dominant scientific knowledge base constructed by Western institutions of higher education, which serves as an important mechanism of white supremacy (Seawright, 2014; Wagner & Yee, 2011).

In higher education, the worldview of the rational, white, male subject is secured and promoted as *the understanding* of all things (Kincheloe, 1999; Pease, 2011). Allen (2001) is careful to point out that the term *whiteness* is not used to describe this global system of white supremacy, "because [whiteness] is a less overtly political term that avoids the fact that the racism of middle-class whites is not peripheral to white supremacy but rather its central demographic" (p. 477). The failure of our institutions and systems to recognize and deal with systemic racism, alongside a belief in the meritocracy of the capitalist system, are key to the survival of the white elite class in maintaining the status quo and, more importantly, propagating the system of white supremacy (Bishop, 2005; Henry & Tator, 2010; Seawright, 2014).

Canada's political, social, and economic institutions are based on Western, European ideas and thought, which are heavily steeped in processes of whiteness, racialization, and white supremacy (Thobani, 2007). The overarching reach of European imperial expansion began during the 16th and 17th centuries and continued through to the mid-20th century, extending to places around the world in Asia,

Africa, and the Americas (Henry & Tator, 2010), and provided the basis for Western/ white political and economic dominance. The Age of Imperialism was a time when relatively developed nations—mostly European nations, but also Japan—were taking over less developed areas by colonizing them, in order to expand their own power and economic opportunities. Today, Canada promotes a nationalist discourse that denies this history of colonization through state mechanisms such as multiculturalism, which provides the appearance of accepting people from different ethnic backgrounds while largely ignoring the country's historic and ongoing role in oppressing Aboriginal Peoples. This denial of Canada's history is accomplished through white supremacy, but in everyday institutional practice, it is accomplished through the strategies and processes of whiteness that are presented to all as fair, neutral, and value-free, by assuming, for instance, that systems and institutions are colour-blind and no structural biases exist that advantage white people. It is presumed that everyone has the same and equal chance at succeeding and accessing the benefits offered by the socioeconomic system and institutions regardless of race. Yet one must examine the concept of white supremacy in order to be able to better see how whiteness ideology is carried out. Shick (2012) defines white supremacy as:

> a practice of how to perform white racial knowledge in a way that manages to hold up a favorable image of whites to themselves while simultaneously reinforcing universal white privilege as a naturalized entitlement. Reasserting white space is a performative act that accomplishes white supremacy and white identity; it also demonstrates and confirms the white racial knowledge on how to do this. White racial knowledge limits and defines what whites are prepared to hear about a subordinate and still "allow a self-concept of innocence to continue." (p. 13)

Thus, Shick provides the processual explanation of how it is difficult for white people to discuss racism and, in particular, why white people fail to see how racism is operating within institutional structures. Other scholars have noted whites' active and passive roles in perpetuating racism; for example, Brown (2009) argued that "whites often benefit from the persistence of whiteness ideologies, but they are also active agents of White supremacy and passive participants in its rewards" (p. 203). Hence, there is a need to locate any understanding about whiteness in the historical and present context of white supremacy.

SOCIAL SERVICE AGENCIES AS STATE STRUCTURES

Since the early 19th century, immigration to the "New World" in North America, along with rapid industrial growth in a burgeoning capitalist economy, created great wealth for a few and great poverty for many, prompting questions about how society was to meet the needs of those who were living in poverty and poor conditions (Lundy, 2004). Deployment of strategies and practices of whiteness have been identified within the responses of social workers and, more importantly, the state structures that developed in tandem with the rise, and evolving role and purpose, of the social work profession. The early responses of the social work profession were established through the Charity Organization Society (COS) and the Settlement House movements (Haynes & White, 1999; Lundy, 2004). The philosophy of the COS was rooted in the idea that individuals can help themselves if all in society were to help one another. While the Settlement House movement also believed in social responsibility, its proponents disagreed with the charity efforts of the COS movement and felt that the COS hid the reality of poverty from the public. Instead, the Settlement House movement believed in developing specific programs that would meet the needs of the community as opposed to developing methods that focused on personal responsibility (Haynes & White, 1999). Nonetheless, both the COS and the Settlement House movements sought the support of the elite and the middle class—the very classes whose positions were based on structural class inequality and its relationship to capitalism.

The idea of helping one another was promoted by privileged, white, middle-class women and the Christian church. Steeped in the colonial history of white supremacy, their perspective and values played an important role in shaping the system itself. These white women viewed themselves as charitable givers who offered acts of kindness to those in need. Roger (2000) draws on this historical legacy to explicate how Western white women today benefit greatly from the professionalization of helping work.

Evidence to support the idea that the COS movement is rooted in white supremacy can be shown in the three principles upon which this approach was founded. First, the COS established a registry that identified those who they deemed to be worthy of "charity" (Lundy, 2004). This registry system granted power to the COS social workers by creating a system of social control over the "other" (Lundy, 2004). The COS strongly believed that the public and government should not intervene in a system that its volunteer practitioners should direct (Haynes & White, 1999). Their specific practices are evident in Mary Richmond's (1861–1928) book, *Friendly Visiting among the Poor*, a manual that set out the social work case method, a system that is still in place in many social service agencies. The aim and focus of the social work case method was to create individual change or personal adaptation as the solution to the ill effects of the capitalist system amongst those living in poverty (Lundy, 2004). The casework method also emphasized the skills and techniques required by those practising the profession. Second, the COS movement "emphasized the principles of administration and efficient organization or otherwise known as 'scientific philanthropy' based on a rational approach of investigation, cooperation, education and coordination" (Haynes & White, 1999, p. 385). The "scientific" premise of this approach was in alignment with the cultural and social processes of whiteness. As noted by Kincheloe (1999),

> Whiteness took shape around the European Enlightenment's notion of rationality with its privileged construction of a transcendental white, male, rational subject who operated at the recess of power while giving every indication that he escaped the confines of time and space. In this context, whiteness was naturalized as a universalized entity that operated as more than mere ethnic personality. (p. 164)

In other words, the white, male, rational subject itself is never under scrutiny for the power that it holds and maintains over the racialized "other." The hidden power of the white, male, heterosexual, able-bodied person in interpreting the social, political, and economic life worlds of the "other" is rarely the focus of discussion. This is because the "other" is subject to the imperialist gaze and rule of white, male, rational scientific thought. The "other" is to be controlled and made to fit within the social order of the capitalist system. Third, the "charity workers firmly believed that the application of specific, transmissible methods and techniques could solve problems previously considered unsolvable" (Haynes & White, 1999, p. 385).

A present-day example of conventional social work practice that supports the advancement and development of purportedly neutral methods and techniques is evidence-based practice. From an anti-racist and anti-oppressive perspective, these methods and techniques are often revealed to be oppressive to service users. For example, in child welfare, Strega and Carriere (2009) emphasize three ways in which social work practice is oppressive toward service users. First, social workers often do not see the power differentials between themselves and service users. Second, social workers often "follow the technical response of the workplace" (p. 15). Third, social workers often fail to examine how their own biases and values affect their choices, decisions, and actions with service users.

Given that the history of the social work profession and methods used in social work practice are heavily steeped in whiteness and white supremacy, one must explore how the organizational contexts for social work practice will also invisibly reproduce forms of white dominance. Any approach to conducting research in this area must pay attention to the insidious ways in which research examining institutional practices will unintentionally reproduce the status quo without a critical understanding of who can be known, what can be known, and what is the history of everyone's knowledge-making and understanding.

A METHODOLOGICAL APPROACH TO CHALLENGING WHITE SUPREMACY IN THE WORKPLACE

The ability to deconstruct racial categories is dependent upon researchers being able to identify the operation of white supremacy in the everyday workplace culture of social service agencies. Black American scholars have studied the ways in which white supremacy has bolstered the white identity, and ideologies and cultural practices, of white people, particularly within institutional structures (Crenshaw, 1991; Dubois, 1935, 1969, 1970). In this fourth wave of race research, rather than just naming cultural differences and reifying racial categories (see Friedman, this volume), critical race scholars are interested in applying theoretical frameworks, such as anti-Black racism or Indigenous worldviews, in order to expose the connections between ideology, policy, and research (Arai & Kivel, 2009). Often, researchers err by assuming that revealing racism is about locating oneself in another person's experience, when addressing white supremacy in research is about "critically engag[ing] his or her own experience as part of the knowledge search" (Dei & Johal, 2005, p. 2). Those who are experiencing exclusion must be the creators of their own knowledge, rather than the mere subjects of research. This approach inevitably demands that those in dominant power positions make visible the ways in which they are reproducing colonizing practices that, at first glance, seem innocent. Researchers cannot expect to address white supremacy if they are unable to realize how seemingly innocent practices of "helping" in fact produce and reproduce colonial relations of domination.

Arai and Kivel (2009) point out that qualitative research has tended to focus on the "process" rather than the "outcome" of racist experiences. Such research has had the effect of re-inscribing the differences of the "other," rather than politicizing the issue and challenging the dominant social order to accept its culpability and responsibility for collectively upholding a system that reproduces white supremacy. As Kivel, Johnson, and Scraton (2009) note, "it is not the race or gender or sexuality of the individual that we need to understand per se, but rather the ideologies and social and cultural practices that emerge in and through these categories of identity and how they converge to afford—or constrain—opportunities" (p. 489). A few examples follow, showing how seemingly neutral, fair, and bias-free institutional values reproduce a culture of white supremacy in the workplace.

In social service agencies, the social and administrative structure of the workplace, at a systemic level, creates and maintains advantages for those who come from a place of whiteness. For example, people rarely question why senior management positions in social service agencies are dominated by white men and, more recently, by white women. Instead, such patterns are largely taken for granted and seen as inevitable. Two common rationalizations are often provided to justify the presence of white men in positions of power: First, the best qualified person must be hired for the position; and, second, not enough qualified Black or Aboriginal individuals apply for such jobs. No one asks why there are no qualified Black or Aboriginal people to apply, or whether the method of determining who is qualified unfairly discounts the skills and abilities of the racialized or Aboriginal people who do apply. A system that continuously favours white people, by placing them in positions of institutional power, will also continue to produce negative outcomes for people of colour and Aboriginal Peoples (Baskin, 2011;

Galabuzi, 2006). The persistent existence of racism ultimately creates a narrative that faults racialized people for not being as successful in employment as white people. Very few people question the ideology of the social and administrative structure of the workplace for applying norms and standards that align with the values of white culture. Most people fail to question or notice the root cause of these inequalities and instead justify and rationalize the taken-for-granted, everyday practices of the workplace.

To identify and document white culture's normative values is a necessary research task, and one that must be marked in the same way that the racial "other" is marked. In other words, white people also need to be racialized in order to reveal how their experiences (re)produce colonial dominance over the "other." One methodological approach to challenge the power of whiteness is to scrutinize the dominant culture's hidden assumptions and values that operate at the institutional level of social service agencies. To do so is methodologically important because those who are in dominant positions must be shown how his or her own knowledge perspective is implicated in reaffirming the current power base. Another benefit to examining the deployment of whiteness strategies in the workplace is to expose the oft-hidden ideas, beliefs, and values of the dominant culture. Once exposed, the dominant culture—and those who promote whiteness—is now potentially able to engage in a dialogue with other worldviews and address built-in white supremacist values. Clearly, the resistance and inability of those in positions of influence to share power will be a major obstacle to challenging institutional power, which also explains why systemic change is a difficult area to tackle in social service agencies' organizational cultures.

In fact, this is why the change management literature often emphasizes the need to gain buy-in from those who are in positions of power before any institutional actions can take place within organizational cultures (Adams & Chandler, 2004; Horwath & Morrison, 2000; Schuman, Lynch, & Abraham, 2005). A white supremacist culture, when challenged, elicits defensiveness that can manifest in several ways. Directions and questions tend to flow downward in a hierarchical organizational structure; this is designed to protect the people in power and their values and views. Criticism or questioning of power is not tolerated, and institutional mechanisms are set in place to deal with people who do not conform. Ideas that challenge those in positions of power are seen as threatening, and a lot of energy is spent ensuring that powerful people are not questioned or challenged. White people spend a lot of time defending themselves against charges of racism. The defensiveness of the powerful creates an oppressive culture. To undo white supremacist culture, respectful expression of conflict needs to be embraced. Organizations need to be able to engage in a dialogue where they can work through this conflict. Several strategies to do so may be used. One might expose the link between defensiveness and fear of losing power; explore and confront white privilege; name defensiveness as a problem; and address the way in which resistance to new ideas subverts the very mission of the organization.

Some change management authors (e.g., Blanchard, 2010; Yee, Wong, & Schlabitz, 2014) have noted that organizations reflect an ideological bias that supports a particular combination of vision, goals, and actions, which, in turn, direct the strategic plan, processes, and systems of the organization. Currently, in many social service agencies, the vision is based on senior management's decisions and relies on outcome measures, which are focused on revenue generation and/or cost-saving measures and, more significantly, are formulated with little consultation or input from those who deliver the actual program (Aronson & Smith, 2010; Yee et al., 2014). The result is that there is little regard for the unintended systemic consequences on the frontline, either the service recipients or the service providers. If an organization were to truly tackle the entrenched forms of white supremacy within its institutional practices, it would devise feedback loops and internal institutional mechanisms that would allow both service providers and those receiving the services to provide input into these higher-level decision-making processes (Yee et al., 2014). This would result in greater transparency and accountability, incorporate open-process mechanisms that can serve as checks and balances on internal systems, and encourage collaborative decision making by those who work in the organization and those who use the organization's services. Ultimately, senior management positions exist in the organization to oversee and ensure the quality of support and relevance of services that are provided to their users. Yet, due to white supremacy, those who work in institutions often deploy strategies of whiteness in order to dominate, control, and oppress the "other," whether this refers to those within the internal organizational culture or those receiving services.

CONCLUSION

In sum, research that is conducted on the institutional structures of social service agencies must take into consideration the concepts of whiteness, racialization, and white supremacy. Failing to do so can only result in a postcolonial approach that simply assumes colonialism has ended (Hart, 2009). Until Indigenous knowledge systems and other life worldviews are allowed a foothold within institutional systems, the system of white supremacy that undergirds Western, European thought will continue to prevail with its harmful and destructive effects of colonizing other life worldviews. Institutions carry values, and until systemic practices of white supremacy are exposed and removed from the institutional structures of social service agencies, the strategies and processes of whiteness will continue to prevail as *the understanding* of all things.

7 | A Research Design for the "Messy Actualities" of Restructured Social Work

Kristin Smith, Associate Professor, School of Social Work, Ryerson University

In the following chapter, I describe a research design I used to explore the knowledge and subjectivities that activists, or anti-oppressive (AOP) social workers, bring to their practice during a time of workplace and social change. The term *subjectivities* refers to all of the conscious and unconscious thoughts and emotions that can account for the relationship between an individual and the social institutions around them (Weedon, 1987). Examples of social institutions can include families, schools, faith-based communities, and pop culture, to name a few. Through discourses, or the language through which ideas are circulated, we learn the proper ways for being in the world, according to what each social institution maintains is true and good (Weedon, 1987). The resulting "subject positions," or ways of being an individual, may not always be compatible, and sometimes we learn that we can choose between them.

The term *activist social worker* is used to refer to those within the profession who draw on feminist, anti-racist, anti-oppressive, and other critical theories in order to link "the personal and the political" (Hick & Pozzuto, 2005, p. x). Baines (2011b) describes the activist practitioner as one who sees him- or herself as an instrument of social change, someone who is engaged in "a much bigger and longer-term effort towards society-wide social justice" (p. 92). Activist social workers seek not only better ways to understand the world but also how to change it based on the principles of social and economic justice. My research on activist social workers sought to understand what happens to these aspirations for social justice when anti-oppression practice approaches are confronted with a new workplace order that is characterized by diminished resources and other constraints.

My research participants all have extensive work experience—ten years or more—in either the child welfare or the primary health care system in Ontario. Both of these sectors have been restructured over several decades through government-led cuts to services and the reorganization of service provision aimed at cost-containment through "efficiencies." These shifts are known as neoliberal restructuring (Baines, 2004a, 2004b, 2007; Dominelli, 1999). Moreover, neoliberal restructuring can also be viewed as the state shifting its obligations for social welfare onto the shoulders of "responsible" and "rational" individuals (Lemke, 2001, p. 201).

My interest in social workers' responses to neoliberal restructuring developed over 18 years of work experience in social and health services in Southern Ontario. In earlier research, I investigated for possibilities of "resistance" by frontline workers who were troubled by the erosion of social programs during the 1990s. I found that social workers' stories revealed a puzzling mix of accommodation practices and hidden oppositional activities (Smith, 2007). Developments in Marxist theory helped to explain the presence of worker agency in the face of structural barriers in the workplace (Edwards, 1979; Hodson, 1995). Labour process theory offered more complex accounts for the ways that workers' subjectivities could shape their oppositional practices (Jermier, Knights, & Nord, 1994; Knights & McCabe, 2000). However, I was left with questions about the contradictions found in social workers' practices within these changing contexts. Why is it that social workers can, at times, deploy creative and innovative tactics to bypass and undermine oppressive policies? Yet these same "resisters" will simultaneously engage in practices that seem highly compliant, obedient, and sometimes even contrary to the needs of service users and their own interests as workers. I was curious about how to make better sense of social workers' accounts, especially when tensions exist between what they imagine themselves to be and what they have to do in order to hold onto their jobs.

As I began to share my earlier research, I noticed that many activist social workers, especially students, were drawn to the findings that revived resistance. It seemed that this particular aspect of my research resurrected an important image for those who harboured strong desires to confront government cuts. Over time, I came to highlight this image in my findings: the "activist hero" who could, even under highly constraining conditions, find ways to "fight back" and "protect" the social advances gained through the welfare state. Admittedly, the positive reactions to these popular images prompted feelings of excitement and pleasure for me as a new researcher. Yet, from a methodological point of view, I was troubled by the ease with which the inconsistencies in social workers' lives were being ironed out of my findings. Over time, my research dilemma turned into a desire to tell a different story about activist social workers struggling in neoliberal contexts. As a result, I set out to explore the knowledge, subjectivities, and work performances that activist social workers bring to their practice when tensions exist between the attachments, desires, and aspirations of the activist social work self and what that self must do every day to get by.

Moving away from static conceptions of identity and subjectivity, my current research approach tries to emphasize the tensions found in new work discourses, and how identity formation (such as activist social worker) and work performances (including those in constrained workplaces) can work simultaneously together and/or against each other. As Leonard (2003) observes, neoliberal discourses—such as those found in restructured social and health service organizations—can be embraced, negotiated, contested, and even rewritten by social workers who are variously positioned within competing discourses, some of which may be autobiographical, cultural, and social. In other words, Leonard argues, for any given individual, a whole range of identity formations or subject positions are simultaneously at play, and some of these positions may serve to bolster the dominant discourses of work, while others may destabilize and undermine them. My intention for this chapter is to share how I used a series of analytic concepts and practical methods in order to capture the fluidity and complexity of AOP social workers' identities and knowledge as they go about the work of helping others in a practice context that is fraught with tensions and contradictions. In doing so, I hope to challenge other AOP researchers to design projects in which they can *sit with* the complexities of identity formation in order to capture the challenges and tensions facing AOP practitioners as they work day-to-day for social change.

My research included a series of in-depth interviews with 17 self-identified activist social workers. The central question I explore through this research is this: How do activist social workers "make themselves up" (Hacking, 2002, p. 99) in relation to their sense of purpose, identities, and experiences of contradictions at work, especially when tensions arise between who they imagine themselves to be as activists and what it is that they must do every day to get by?

Theoretically, my research question is rooted in Foucault's (1991) ideas about governmentality. Governmentality directs my attention away from state power and the idea that policies are imposed on people from above, to instead focus on the ways in which strategies for shaping the conduct of people operate through people's day-to-day practices. These processes are what Foucault (1994) calls "techniques of the self" (p. 87). Techniques of the self include all the multiple ways that individuals will experience, understand, judge, and organize their own behaviour or performances of self.

The idea of discourse is central to governmentality studies. Foucault (1991) saw discourses as sets of socially arranged rules or guides which, at a given period and for a given society, define the statements we are allowed to make—"the limits and forms of the sayable" (p. 59). Davies (2000) explains that the concept of "positioning" (p. 70) is central to an understanding of the ways in which people are constituted through and within discourse. How we position ourselves in discourses is constantly open to shifts and changes. As Davies explains, "who I am potentially shifts with each speaking, with each moment of being" (p. 71).

In addition to describing the methods of research that I have used to explore my central question, my aim for this chapter is to identify and discuss various theoretical quandaries that I encountered while assembling these methods. I anticipated being able to share how I resolved these quandaries in my research process. However, I have since discovered that this is not an easily accomplished task, and perhaps it is not one that is entirely possible. Nor am I convinced that this is a desirable end point. Instead, I have chosen to focus on the value that these methods provide because of their capacity to highlight the uncertainties, the inconsistencies, and the "messiness" of participants' actual everyday work lives.

HOW DO SOCIAL WORKERS "MAKE THEMSELVES UP"?

By design, my research question signals an ongoing critical interrogation that can never be definitively resolved. Following Foucault (2000), I am asking of activist social workers, "what are we in this particular moment?" (p. 216); how are we making ourselves up now? Behind these queries lies the suggestion that the human subject has limited reflexivity, that there is always an interpretation that can be incomplete or one that could be possibly contested. This suggestion can be deeply troubling for some researchers working from an anti-oppressive perspective because of the strong desire to integrate the experiences of community members in a way that highlights the knowledge of those members (Greene & Chambers, 2011). Yet the idea that people's insights, interpretations, and narratives about themselves are limited and incomplete was simply assumed in my other life as a practising—non-academic— social worker. During my informal, everyday interaction with colleagues in social service workplaces, it was a common occurrence that we did not take each other's accounts of work completely at face value. It was a given expectation that we would disagree, interpret things differently, or wonder silently about how "hidden agendas" and "personal baggage" played out in people's perceptions and decision making in their social work practice.

However, in the field of AOP qualitative research, it is quite another thing to problematize the idea that research participants are reflexive agents in relation to their identities and experiences of workplace change. Discomfort abounds when questions are asked about whether research participants are always able to give a "valid" and "trustworthy" account of their reasons for doing the things that they do as social workers. Hollway and Jefferson (2000) call this the "transparent self problem" (p. 3), and explain that the discomfort is rooted in the assumption found in many qualitative research traditions whereby it is believed that research participants are always "telling it like it is" (p. 2). However, as these authors point out, even if we accept at face value everything that our research participants tell us, are we satisfied that we have been told everything that is relevant? What assumptions do we make about the effect of people's motives, memory, and investments on their narratives? What effect do I have as an interviewer on the answers given to me? How do gender, sex, race, age, class, and other identity markers intersect with each other and also with the answers that are given, and the interpretations that are made? And, finally, what are we as researchers to do when the answers we are given, however limited and incomplete, are also riddled with inconsistencies and contradictions?

From a research perspective, my question *questions* the existence of a unitary and knowledgeable subject, and, therefore, it contains both epistemological and ethical implications. Who am I to challenge whether others always know why they are doing what they are doing when they do it? As Scott (1992) observes, "what could be truer, after all, than a subject's own account of what he or she has lived through?" (p. 24). However, as Scott rightly points out, when we are talking about "experience" in these ways, we are led to take for granted the existence of experienced individuals who have knowledge-generating capacities. She explains:

> When experience is taken as the origin of knowledge, the vision of the individual subject (the person who had the experience or the historian who recounts it) becomes the bedrock of evidence upon which the explanation is built. Questions about the constructed nature of experience, about how subjects are constituted as different in the first place, about how one's vision is structured—about language (or discourse) and history—are left aside. (p. 25)

Scott makes the point that our research subjects' unquestioned accounts, along with our desires to pin down these accounts as "real," results in knowledge that is likely to *hide* more than it reveals. Therefore, for the purposes of my research, I am particularly interested in finding this "left aside" knowledge about which Scott speaks—the "messy actualities" of "what actually happens" (O'Malley, Weir, & Shearing, 1997, p. 509) in my research subjects' dealings with changes in their workplaces. How do I create space and opportunity in participant interviews to allow room for this hidden knowledge to emerge? How do I capture accounts that are inconsistent? What kinds of methods enable me to see the contingencies upon which are based my research participants' expectations, desires, and feelings about their work practices and identities (Hoggett, 2001)? Chris Weedon (1987), along with other feminist poststructuralists (Butler, 1990; Davies, 2000; Scott, 1992), argues that we can extend our readings of subjects' accounts with the following idea:

> How we live our lives as conscious thinking subjects, and how we give meaning to the material social relations under which we live and with which we structure our everyday lives, depends on the range and social power of existing discourses, our access to them and the political strength of the interests which they represent. (p. 26)

I understand Weedon to mean that our existence as persons, and the patterns of desires that we take to be key indicators of our essential selves, are reflections of the discourses and subject positions that are made available to us. Through these discourses, we are constituted, and through them we constitute ourselves.

Taking up ideas about the discursive production of subject positions, Bansel, Davies, Gannon, and Linnell (2008) examine their everyday practices within educational institutions in order to consider how they position themselves as appropriate subjects in the context of a neoliberal, productivity audit–driven culture. These authors explain that "discursive analysis" (p. 675) draws attention to the ways that discourse works on, and through, people to produce not only particular kinds of subjects, but also the actions that they engage in and the feelings that they experience. Noting that these actions and feelings tend to be seen as reflections of "real selves" (p. 675) rather than of discourses, these authors suggest that attention should be shifted away from the individual speaking subject, and instead focused on the various discourses at work, thus enabling both the visibility and interrogation of the constituting power of discourses. Butler (1997) similarly suggests that it is important not to conflate the individual or the person with "the subject" (p. 10). The subject, she explains, rather than being identified strictly with the individual, ought to be designated as a category or a "placeholder" (p. 10) that individuals have historically come to occupy, but will also change over time and place.

In the following excerpt from my research transcript, I apply the idea of positioning in discourse in order to demonstrate how Didi, a primary health care social worker, has been constituted through neoliberal discourses at work. Where once Didi would have used her professional judgement to determine the amount of time spent with a client, she now describes the pressures she feels to make more "efficient" use of her time. To ignore these pressures, in Didi's mind, is to risk losing her job. She explains how these fears have come to shape her practice:

> I do 50 minute sessions, ten minutes of what they now call "collateral time" at the end of that 50 minutes in which you are supposed to do a note. ... I mean it is down to a science. You get ten more additional minutes for each client at the end of the day to do notes, and that's it.

Didi's account resonates powerfully with what it means to become a neoliberal subject (Davies, 2005). However, Bansel and colleagues' (2008) suggestion to "turn away" from the individual speaking subject raises ethical and political questions for me as a researcher who is expected to interpret another person's positioning. Specifically, I am concerned about how such a "turning away" from the individual speaking subject can potentially activate a misuse of power and authority in the social and textual relations between the AO researcher and the researched participant (Gonick & Hladki, 2005). For example, in this same interview, I asked Didi how she felt about the shifts in her practice. She described at length the intense anxiety she experiences based on a belief that her new work practices conflict with her values and commitments to social justice. She also shared various ways she manages to continue her commitments to social justice by working *around* the new policies. By only attending to workplace discourses about the need to ration care, I would have missed Didi's description of the many ways she resists these pressures, including fiddling with case notes and misleading her employer about the number of clients she sees. As a result, I see the importance of ensuring that my research practices are ethically responsible in that I represent the complexity in people's lives—that there is both "reciprocity" through the mutual negotiation of meaning *and* "validity" resulting from the trustworthiness of the "data" (Lather, 1991, p. 57).

Hoggett, Beedell, Jimenez, Mayo, and Miller (2006) attempt to address the tensions between a discursive reading of the subject and an understanding that subjects do have agency. In order to highlight tensions, these authors developed a psychosocial approach to interviewing live subjects, which seeks to understand how internal psychological factors and external social factors interact. A psychosocial approach, according to Hoggett et al. (2006), requires detailed interviews in which the researcher seeks personal stories from participants about their work-related roles. It is through these personal stories that the researcher can reveal work-related dilemmas and the various ways that different professionals respond to them: "a source of despair for one, a source of fascination and an opportunity for learning for another" (pp. 691–692). Based on their findings, the authors argue that an individual can adopt a variety of work-related subject positions including refusal, identification, dis-identification, perversion, corruption, and even a transformation of the position itself.

Drawing on Hoggett et al.'s (2006) ideas about a psychosocial approach to research design, I developed interview formats that would intentionally draw out personal, biographical stories, in addition to social workers' perceptions about tensions related to the changing nature of their work. For example, I came to understand that Didi's expressions of profound sadness and guilt over her sense of loss in terms of opportunities for social justice–based practice were deeply related to her powerful attachments to a family history woven with injustice and painful events. As she explains, her working-class parents never had the opportunities afforded to her, and this knowledge has always motivated her to rectify the hardships faced in their lives, as well as for others who struggle at the margins.

In addition to using methods for understanding how biographical histories interact with workplace discourses, I found it helpful to borrow from Hoggett's (2001) suggestion that the self is not unitary but rather a number of selves who are often in conflict with each other. Hoggett emphasizes that this model of the subject is not intended to imply that the idea of identity is a slippery illusion. Rather, it points to processes whereby people create coherent narratives about their lives in ways that are reflective of the many discourses they live through. It is important to recognize how these narratives can both sustain people in the present and provide a guide for navigating the future. At the same time, Hoggett (2001) points out that our capacity to be reflective agents is often constrained by the difficulties we encounter in facing our own fears and anxieties: "Some ideas and experiences are just too painful to think about, even with the support and solidarity of others, and they therefore get split off" (p. 42).

Hoggett also observes that reflectivity often requires courage and, at times, people may lack the courage to think certain things about themselves and others. Perhaps, suggests Hoggett, we need to contain our tendency to equate agency with constructive forms of managing at work. He observes, "Just as we can be destructive agents so also at times we can be constructive in our dependency and powerlessness" (2001, p. 43). Drawing on Hoggett's work has encouraged me to design methods of research with live subjects that make room for non-reflective as well as reflective forms of agency, for acting on impulse as well as conscious, intentional choice-making.

THE DEFENDED SUBJECT

Hollway and Jefferson (2000) explain that the concept of the defended subject allows a researcher to attend to how and where subjects may become invested in particular positions within discourses in order to protect vulnerable aspects of the self against the discomforts associated with contradictions that they encounter in their daily lives. In other words, the defended subject allows for an understanding both of the effects of social discourses and the unique emotional defences found in the stories that people tell about themselves. For example, understanding activist social workers as defended subjects enables me to see the ways that their positioning mobilizes discourses of innocence in the face of child welfare and primary health care restructuring. The following excerpt from an interview with Frank, a child welfare supervisor, demonstrates some of the ways that social workers can manage to defend themselves from complicity with harm done to service users. In this part of our discussion, Frank is reflecting on the damaging effects of narrow risk assessment tools adopted in Ontario during the late 1990s:

> Frank: I think the more we reflect on what we've done in the risk assessment days, the more I think we're starting to realize how rigid we were. It's easy for us to remind ourselves that we made the best choices we could, and we really did, you know. I've even likened it to historically where social work has made shifts around the residential schools in the 50s and 60s ... some of the people teaching us to be social workers were actually social workers at that time. They believed that they were doing the best service they could for Aboriginal children ... and then, you know, came the regrets.

> Kristin: How do you think we are implicated in that? What do we do to make up for that, to atone, to be accountable?

> Frank: Now I'm starting to feel a little defensive here.

> Kristin: Can you talk about that?

> Frank: I was quite new to the job when risk assessment fell onto our laps and we were all trained to use it. So like, in terms of accountability, I kind of feel like, okay, I was trained by the university, I got lucky to get a job, and then the risk assessment model came in, and it is certainly contrary to what we were trained to do. So I manufactured my own practice with the structure I was given and I enjoyed working with families and their children. I just had to work within the system as it was ... how much am I responsible for that?

Frank's closing question reflects an innocence that is grounded in the belief that he is non-complicit with the negative effects of his workplace restructuring. Flax (1993) describes this kind of innocent knowledge as an unwavering belief in some sort of moral truth that can guide us in the world:

> Those whose actions are grounded in or informed by such truth will also have their innocence guaranteed. They can do only good, not harm, to others. They act as servants of something higher and outside (or more than) themselves, their own desires, and the effects of their particular histories or social locations. (p. 133)

Davies (2000) points out that, within neoliberalism, people must rely on illusions of autonomy in order to ensure successful adaptation to whatever new circumstances are presented. Much like Frank, it is possible that other social workers draw on this illusion of autonomy as a defence that allows them to position themselves as beyond the reach of regressive policies and oppressive practices in the workplace. Paradoxically, social workers may also position themselves as constrained by those same policies but miraculously find ways to stand out as exceptions from the collective—the "heroes who engage in specific tasks and conquer the difficulties that the world puts in their way" (Davies, 2000, p. 56).

As I conducted interviews with social workers, I became more adept at paying close attention to discourses and practices as they appear in social work subjects' talk about themselves, their life-histories, and their experiences at work (Bansel et al., 2008). According to Bansel and colleagues (2008), this is a research method for listening to people's stories that tries to avoid the fragmentation and decontextualization that can occur with the more traditional methods found in qualitative studies. I should emphasize that my "method," following Foucault's (2000) own claims, is not closed or in any way finished. As Davies (2005) observes about researching the discursive, this is a "realm not readily pinned down with words, not readily amenable to logic and rationality" (p. 13). Throughout the writing up of my research, I have paid particular attention to the fluid nature of discourse. Yet at the same time, it has been important for me to find ways to anchor social workers' life-stories within discourses—to take strategic snapshots, if you will—so that I can research and productively write about the details of social workers' lives. I have found that such strategic views of the subject enable me to see how it is that social workers make themselves up in the changing context of work. Working from this point of view, I have organized the final sections of this chapter to address the following question: Who did I recruit to my study?

WHO ARE MY RESEARCH PARTICIPANTS? SHATTERING IDENTITY MARKERS

As I set out to write a description of my research participants, I became aware of my urge to present them to the reader using conventional identity markers, such as those typically found within qualitative research. Gonick and Hladki (2005) describe this conventional approach as the "grid of identities, similitudes and analogies" (p. 289) that researchers rely on in order to sort out differences and similarities in their research. These authors explain that conventional methods for introducing research participants usually include a series of ready-made, familiar, identifying categories such as race, gender, class, ethnicity, age, and so forth. People are assumed to belong to these categories in an uncomplicated and straightforward way. For different reasons, AOP research tends to reproduce these categories of meaning. AOP uses identity markers as a way to instill value in, and recognize, social difference. However, I was troubled by how much of my research participants' lives were hidden or ironed out by these methods of categorization. By contrast, when reading through my transcripts, I was struck by how my participants' lives literally spilled over the edges of these ready-made categories. Gonick and Hladki (2005) argue that relying on such practices reaffirms uncritical assumptions about traditional identity categories. Those categories are assumed to represent an "authentic voice" (p. 290), and we are distracted from questioning how they were produced in the first place. Gonick and Hladki caution researchers about the hazards of reproducing the exclusions and marginalizations of research subjects who speak from outside the imagined authenticity: "In the same moment that difference is named, it is also contained" (p. 290). Capturing the pressure I felt to produce these conventional inventories, Gonick and Hladki explain that such an approach dissipates anxiety because while difference is acknowledged through this technique of containment, it is also made commensurable. In other words, pinning things down provides a "zone of comfort" (p. 291) for both the writer and the readers of research.

Yet, as I read through my interview transcripts over and over again, one thing was made abundantly and consistently clear: The actual lived lives of my research participants rarely conformed to the comforts of my initial summaries. Instead, participants' accounts of themselves revealed complicated intersections, fluidities, overlappings, and inconsistencies that cannot be contained within the simplistic and predetermined categories of identity. As Sin and Yan (2003) explain, "positioning difference is relational depending on the particularity of the social, cultural, and political context. We are multi-positioned, implicated in unequally empowered ways of understanding and doing. Our social positions are entangled and simply cannot be defined by a set of binaries" (p. 33). I take from this critique of AOP that my research subjects are never fixed, but are instead fluid subjects. I must remember that my research subjects are constantly at work on themselves within conditions that are often beyond their control and that are endlessly shifting. Given their multiple and complicated positionings, how then can I introduce my research subjects to the reader of this chapter in a way that does justice to the complexities of their lives?

Taking up the questions about how research participants become knowable in research writing, Gonick and Hladki (2005) draw on Foucault's notion of "heterotopia" in order to think through ways for representing the space that resides "outside of safe and secure means of knowing" (p. 288). Foucault (1986) describes heterotopias as "counter-sites, a kind of effectively enacted utopia in which the real sites, all the other sites that can be found within the culture, are simultaneously represented, contested, and inverted" (p. 23). Gonick and Hladki work with this idea to see research subjects as paradoxical: "where the logic of naming, of categorizing through division and designation, are shattered" (p. 289). According to these authors, the task for researchers involves exploring the contradictory and ambivalent ways that people come to tell their life stories, recognizing "that they may never be fully known or representable" (p. 291). This involves taking into account how research participants have historically been misrecognized by the identities and categories used by powerful others, while also manoeuvring around the desirable and respectable selves people wish to be, and all of the social, political, and economic constraints that govern their lives. Simply put, the researcher's job is to find "new ways of speaking and listening that both acknowledge difference and work against the othering gaze" (Gonick & Hladki, 2005, p. 293).

"WORKING WITH THE WHOLE" AND PEN PORTRAITS

In order to put Gonick and Hladki's (2005) ideas to work as a method in my research, I borrowed an idea from Hollway and Jefferson (2000) called "working with the whole" (p. 5). According to Hollway and Jefferson, working with the whole of my research data requires that I attend carefully to context, links, and contradictions within that whole. Putting this into practice involved an intensive process of detailed and repeated readings of transcripts. I sought out and identified places in the transcripts where participants positioned themselves in a particular way. Next, I made summaries of the transcripts and highlighted the ways that different positionings were revealed to contain contradictions. I developed a binder for the summaries so that I had easy access to my findings. My binder became a valuable tool as I returned to the summaries countless times throughout the process of writing up my findings.

In order to make full and effective use of the detailed information I had compiled about my research participants' lives, I utilized another concept developed by Hollway and Jefferson (2000), known as "pen portraits" (p. 70). Pen portraits are biographical accounts that reveal, rather than iron out, inconsistencies, contradictions, and puzzles found in the stories people tell about themselves. Using the detailed biographical information provided by my research participants, I created a written "portrait" for each research subject, to be used not only as a source of information for analysis but also as a method for introducing the reader to my research subjects. This method is intended to provide the reader with access to the constituting conditions of participants' lives and work stories, along with the stories they hold onto about how they have come to know themselves as particular kinds of social work subjects over time. The following example of a pen portrait demonstrates how this method can highlight the context and the complexities of people's lives in powerful ways.

I found that writing pen portraits of each of the social workers in my research made the research participants come to life for me as a writer. I used pen portraits as a method in order to provide the reader of my research with a richer and more layered glimpse into the complexities that are woven in, and throughout, social workers' work-life stories. For example, Carrie's pen portrait manages to hold intact what she has described to be important to her during our interviews—significant people, life events, major influences—and, consequently, it reveals various intersections of identities as well as her multiple positionings within competing discourses. For instance, Carrie openly embraces discourses of "Indianness" while also leaning on discourses of whiteness, femininity, and modernity to position herself as "successful" within her workplace. Simultaneously embracing her "Indianness" and distancing herself from her older, more traditional Aboriginal colleagues, she rejects those bodies because she believes they will be positioned as inferior by her white colleagues working off-reserve. Carrie's pen portrait brings to the forefront the impact of racism, pain, loss, and possibly betrayal on the constitution of one's subjectivities. Her emotional description of her mother's death, along with painful accounts of racism confronted in her schooling, provide new openings for thinking about how she has learned to draw on multiple and contradictory subjectivities to position herself as buffered from pain and the material effects of racism in the workplace. As a research method, her pen portrait counters dominant qualitative research tendencies, which force participants into essentialized and totalized units where they are perceived as having little or no internal, historical, or social variation.

CONCLUSION

I believe that the theoretical analysis and methods that I adopted in my research, including discourse analysis, the "defended subject," "working with the whole," and

CARRIE

Carrie is in her late 20s and for the past six years she has worked as a case manager in child welfare at a Native Services branch of a children's aid society in Ontario. Before that time, she worked in a group home for troubled youth. Carrie identifies herself as Aboriginal, frequently invoking the phrase, "I'm an Indian" but, she also notes that her paternal great-grandparents immigrated to Canada from Eastern Europe during the 1930s.

When I asked Carrie about any early influences that led her to social work, she shared some painful stories about her mom's life. She was with her mom each day during her agonizing death from cancer when Carrie was only 19 years old. Carrie was raised by her mom and she identifies her as having played a major role in the development of her own identity, including some of the knowledge she draws on as a social worker. She struggles to put words to what this difficult loss meant for her life:

> She bled to death at home. It was very traumatic. And I think that helps me because you know when people say I am young and yes, I don't have kids, but I can say I have a lot of life experience for being so young...

Carrie shared memories of harsh forms of racism that she encountered during high school where Aboriginal kids were segregated in grade 9 and put into separate classes. This policy was rationalized by the belief that elementary schooling on the reserve, where Carrie's family lived, was of an inferior quality. She explains how the emphasis on difference, the elevation of white students' achievements, and the marginalization of those whom she had previously identified with, all led her to distance herself from her own community. Carrie understood a dynamic where excelling at school meant certain rejection. She describes being taunted: "you're not Native anymore, you speak like a white person." By grade 11, she became known by the other kids as simply "white-washed."

The theme of not fitting in anywhere combined with a desire to erase the past circulates in Carrie's work-life story. She describes her efforts to be seen as "modern" at a time when many members of her community are reclaiming their spiritual and cultural traditions: "I wear eye contacts and dye my hair and I wear makeup." Carrie experiences tensions between herself and some of the older, more traditional women she works with in child welfare on the reserve. She recognizes that Aboriginal social workers are treated differently by white social workers at the main agency in town. She understands that to be a Native Services branch worker entails being defined as one of the "outcast people." However, she notes that her own capacity for upward mobility has improved recently under new changes in child welfare policy. Now, she believes that she offers desirable characteristics because of her ability to "pass as white." As far as workers who "look Aboriginal" are concerned, she confides, "They just aren't taken seriously." When asked if she thinks this will ever change, Carrie makes a sweeping gesture with her arm and says, "the whole Government of Canada ... (laughter) ... It always looks good on paper (laughter)."

pen portraits, have enabled me to better reveal the uneven and varied biographical histories that influence activist social workers, along with the unpredictable and at times tenuous experiences of work within a context of neoliberal governance. O'Malley, Weir, and Shearing (1997) have called this uneven history the "messy actualities" of governance: "In this we refer not only to the recognition of the multiplicity of voices and discourses subject to government but not aligned with it, but equally to the multiplicity of voices within rule itself" (p. 505). Methods that are sensitive to issues of social differences and heterogeneity provide better access to the multiplicity of voices and experiences existing within research participants' accounts of themselves. My use of such methods has been able to extend and expand my readings of people's lives in ways that emphasize paradoxes and inconsistencies in how they make themselves up, and as a result, my findings are able to go beyond the safe and bounded practices of conventional qualitative research.

Section III

Valuing Fluidity and Unknowing

8 | Phenomenology as Social Work Inquiry

Parallels and Divergences with Anti-Oppressive Research

Susan Preston, Associate Professor, School of Social Work, Ryerson University

Lisa Redgrift, Doctoral Student, Department of Sociology and Social Anthropology, Dalhousie University

Current scholarship about anti-oppressive perspectives (AOP) within research tends to focus on exploring oppression or doing research with or about marginalized communities, as the "who, where, and why" of research. However, there is minimal exploration about the "what and how" of such research, which is not surprising as AOP research literature suggests that methods may not follow a traditional research design format (Potts & Brown, 2005); may combine methods (Strier, 2007); may bring historically contradictory approaches together (Fawcett & Hearn, 2004); and may include an evolving research design to more consistently reflect participants' experiences, and an openness to emerging or reconstructed approaches and methods (Potts & Brown, 2005; Strier, 2007). In this context, we consider phenomenology as a form of anti-oppressive social work research.

Phenomenological inquiry can be problematic, mostly due to conflation of its two main approaches: descriptive and interpretive approaches. Alongside this concern, there are potential tensions between phenomenological inquiry and AOP, which may explain why social work research has engaged only minimally with phenomenology. There is a growing interest in how phenomenology and social work may be linked for practice and research (e.g., Newberry, 2012), and our contribution here is intended to add to that emerging discussion. We acknowledge the struggles we encountered in our own work, given the limitations of social work scholarship regarding phenomenology, both as a philosophical foundation and as an approach to research, within an AOP understanding. These struggles and tensions have been the impetus for this chapter, as one attempt to enhance research literacy (Dominelli, 2009). To this end, we explore these tensions and offer beginning ideas about why and how social work research could further engage with phenomenological inquiry to advance the principles and practices of AOP.

UNDERSTANDING PHENOMENOLOGY: DESCRIPTIVE AND INTERPRETIVE APPROACHES TO INQUIRY

Deeply rooted in philosophical traditions (Lopez & Willis, 2004; Starks & Trinidad, 2007), phenomenology aims to examine the lived experiences of humans within a specific context (Wojnar & Swanson, 2007). Phenomenological inquiry is concerned with an individual's experience with a phenomenon through exploring the essence of experience (Kleiman, 2003, 2004; Moustakas, 1994; van Manen, 1997). Descriptive and interpretive phenomenology each have their own foundational tenets, yet often they are fused as if a single methodology, which becomes problematic in terms of the rigour of the research (Giorgi, 2008). Given the key differences between these two approaches, we discuss each of them separately here.

While both forms of phenomenology share an interpretive theoretical paradigm, the perspectives of each approach vary with respect to their view of human experience, specifically regarding context and essence. This is most obvious with respect to how the "life world" of an individual is differentiated between the two approaches. Descriptive phenomenology (developed by Edmund Husserl) attempts to comprehend the meaning of human experience, viewing reality as being embedded in the lived experience of the individual, as something that is independent of context (Giorgi, 2012; Laverty, 2003). Interpretive phenomenology (originated by Martin Heidegger) strives to create understanding through illuminating details within the lived experience by emphasizing the history and context of the individual's experience (Koch, 1995, as cited in Laverty, 2003). Descriptive phenomenology aims to uncover what humans experience before they interpret or reflect upon it as the true essence of a phenomenon (Lopez & Willis, 2004; Moustakas, 1994). Alternatively, the life world in interpretive phenomenology assumes that human reality is always impacted by the world, including social, cultural, and political factors (Lopez & Willis, 2004), and considers social context, culture, and history (Wojnar & Swanson, 2007). The life world as a mechanism of understanding is thus dissimilar between the two approaches.

To more fully understand these two strands of phenomenology, we can examine the unique elements of descriptive phenomenology compared to interpretive phenomenology from four elements of knowledge-building: axiology, epistemology, ontology, and methodology. The axiology of phenomenological inquiry values the lived experience and describes the understanding of the experience, including the values of the researcher (Hart, 1997). In descriptive phenomenology, the experience itself has value; however, in interpretive phenomenology, the meaning of the experience appears to have greater value, perhaps because the lived experience itself is an interpretive process (Dowling, 2007). These axiological differences must be taken into account in any forms of phenomenological inquiry.

Epistemologically, phenomenological inquiry recognizes the meaning of an experience as a justifiable source of knowledge, drawn from how someone lives, interprets, and conceptualizes their own experience (Pietersma, 2000; Westphal, 2003). In descriptive phenomenology, the researcher seeks to limit, neutralize, and counter their influence on the research process, including on the participants, understood as "transcendental subjectivity" (Husserl, 2001, cited in Wojnar & Swanson, 2007, p. 173). However, interpretive phenomenology references "intersubjectivity" (Lopez & Willis, 2004, p. 730) as a way of creating knowledge through the "fusion of horizons" (Gadamer, 1976, cited in Lopez & Willis, 2004, p. 730) between the researcher and the participant. This subtle distinction in knowledge justification thus influences phenomenology's research design.

Phenomenological inquiry's ontology recognizes that one's experience is reflective, subjective, contemplative, and contextual (e.g., Laverty, 2003), and thus reality is "constituted" by what one has experienced. In descriptive phenomenology, each person's reality is constituted in the pre-reflective, non-interpreted lived experience as a form of "radical autonomy" (Lopez & Willis, 2004, p. 728). Conversely, interpretive phenomenology assumes each person's reality is influenced by their relationship with their world, as a form of "situated freedom" (Lopez & Willis, 2004, p. 728). Thus the nature of being is either influenced or not by a person's positionality in the world, depending on one's approach to phenomenology.

In a phenomenological inquiry, methodology is a process that is inductive, iterative, and emerging, whereby the "phenomena dictates [*sic*] method" (Hycner, 1999, as quoted in Groenewald, 2004, p. 9). Within descriptive phenomenology, the principal focus is to gather stories (experiences, beliefs, and feelings) about the phenomenon, allowing for rich descriptions of that experience (Groenewald, 2004). Meanwhile, with interpretive phenomenology, the inquiry itself becomes meaningful partly through a researcher's interpretive approach by means of a reciprocal process between the participant and the researcher (as a hermeneutic circle). As such, the research process varies considerably between the two approaches.

Having explored these core elements of producing knowledge, noting the differences between descriptive and interpretive phenomenology, we now explore both approaches from an AOP perspective.

INTERSECTIONS BETWEEN AOP AND PHENOMENOLOGY THROUGH THE RESEARCH PROCESS

Here we explore phenomenology through an AOP lens, considering ways the two approaches to phenomenological inquiry parallel and contrast with AOP research processes. In the following section, we then narrow our focus to an exploration of specific facets of tensions when creating knowledge through phenomenological inquiry within an AOP framework.

We begin with exploring how the role of the researcher is positioned differently in the two approaches to phenomenological inquiry. Descriptive phenomenology contends that the researcher must abandon prior knowledge and personal biases in order to fully understand the experience in question (Lopez & Willis, 2004; Moustakas, 1994). As transcendental subjectivity, the prior knowledge and personal biases of the researcher are continually assessed and balanced to ensure they do not alter the research. This contrasts somewhat with AOP's critical reflexivity and subject positioning (Heron, 2005), where the researcher would unearth and acknowledge the impact of their worldview and identity, and how that might veil their own influence over the research process. However, we also note that centring the participant as the primary source of knowledge, by limiting the researcher's influence, reflects an AOP commitment to valuing the participant's experience as expert knowledge about the phenomenon (Fook & Gardner, 2007; Ruch, 2005).

Meanwhile, interpretive phenomenology contends that humans are unable to discard their prior knowledge, noting that it often leads them to a particular research topic in the first place (Koch, 1995). As an essential component of the research process, allowances are made to incorporate the knowledge of the researcher as a form of "co-constitutionality" with the participants. In this way, we suggest that interpretive phenomenology is better aligned with AOP research, making the influence of the researcher's role more visible (Harrison, MacGibbon, & Morton, 2001) and promoting a co-construction by the researcher and the participants in interpreting the experience.

Posing a research question can be a negotiation between the researcher's insider status as someone who may have elements of the lived experience similar to the research participants (Humphrey, 2007; Tufford & Newman, 2012), while also being an outsider to the participant experience through being in the researcher role, which can create a power imbalance with the people we research (Humphrey, 2007; Rogers, 2012). Some suggest it is best to not share the central research question with participants, to avoid controlling or directing the inquiry and thus to promote participants' meanings as the interpretation of the experience (Groenewald, 2004). Recognizing the deceptive nature of this practice as contrary to AOP, we consider a slightly different approach. With descriptive phenomenology, withholding the central research question may be important as a way to limit the researcher's influence and thus foreground the participant's pre-interpretive experience, but, from an AOP perspective, this withholding must be clearly articulated to the participants and put forward as a choice for the participant, to minimize the involuntariness inherent in this power dynamic (Rogers, 2012). Withholding the central research question in interpretive phenomenology seems irrelevant, recalling the co-constructing role of the participant and the researcher in this approach. Additionally, it is important that the researcher clearly articulate their experience with and understanding of the phenomenon, as part of the shared interpretive process (Lather, 1991). In this way, interpretive phenomenology brings the participant and researcher together in the process and outcome of the inquiry, and thus may be more closely aligned with an AOP approach (Baines & Edwards, 2015; Rogers, 2012).

We also can consider the sampling and recruitment process in phenomenological inquiry from an AOP perspective. As the study of the essence of the lived experience of individuals with a phenomenon, any approach to "who we are going to involve and how" (Potts & Brown, 2005, p. 269) is informed by seeking participants who have a life history with the phenomenon. In a descriptive approach, which limits the researcher's influence over the process, it may be best to only seek the first participant (whom the researcher may encounter through their own experience with the phenomenon), and then pursue a snowball approach as a means of having insiders "do" the inviting (Potts & Brown, 2005). In this way, potential participants may be drawn to the inquiry through the lived experience of other participants, rather than at the invitation of the researcher. In an interpretive approach, perhaps the researcher may be more directly involved in seeking participants, as the researcher's role is more integrated in the process and the researcher may be seen as an insider. Either of these approaches thus seems complementary to AOP research.

In both approaches to phenomenology, interviews are common forms of data collection to explore the "what" and "how" of the lived experience (Creswell, 2013; Moustakas, 1994; van Manen, 1997). With any form of phenomenological inquiry, we suggest there be very few pre-planned questions in advance of data collection, with additional questions based on the answers provided by participants, to focus the research on the lived experience of the participants (Knox & Burkard, 2009; Kvale, 1996). However, the methods of conducting those interviews and the ensuing analysis have some variation between the two forms of phenomenological inquiry. In descriptive phenomenology, we might anticipate that the researcher attempts to limit their influence in the interview process through a process of bracketing, which can be understood as a purposeful effort to recognize and separate out one's own perceptions, assumptions, biases, and experiences with the phenomenon to more fully focus on the participant's story (Drew, 2004; Gearing, 2004). However, to do so, the researcher may become somewhat detached from the interview process, which seems counter to AOP's recognition of the researcher's presence and influence with every step of any research process (Rogers, 2012; Starks & Trinidad, 2007). We discuss this in more detail in the following section regarding tensions within an AOP approach to phenomenological inquiry. Here we suggest that one approach to minimize researcher influence is to create an interview guide that is very short, with just a couple of broad questions about the phenomenon being studied, and few, if any, probing or secondary questions. Probing might only be done through asking questions such as "Tell me more about that," rather than anything more directive in its intent. In this way, the interview process focuses more on what the participant says and less on what the researcher asks. It also reduces the potential for the researcher to over-influence the interview;

bracketing can allow researchers to "[hold] in abeyance one's preconceptions [that] may engender sensitivity to alternate perspectives thus permitting additional avenues of exploration and allowing apparent contradictions to emerge" (Tufford & Newman, 2012, pp. 90–91).

Interpretive phenomenology may approach interviews differently, recognizing that the researcher cannot be "bracketed out" of the research process. In an interpretive approach, the researcher and the participant co-create the story of the participant's experience of the phenomenon being studied. In this way, we see interpretive phenomenology as more aligned with an AOP approach to research, wherein there is a shared process of "seeking, listening and learning" (Potts & Brown, 2005, p. 271). An interview guide might begin with two broad questions, but also could contain several probing questions within these two broad areas, as well as other questions secondary to the two broad primary questions. Through the use of different styles of interview guides, we suggest that data collection in both descriptive and interpretive phenomenology may fit well within an AOP approach to research.

The process of data analysis can be a challenge, given the openness of phenomenology to focusing on the participant's experience of the phenomenon, in considering how much the evaluation and interpretation of the data might be informed by the researcher's own understandings. In descriptive phenomenology, the analysis process is especially challenging, given the expectations around distancing the researcher. "Descriptive adequacy" (Ashworth, 2000, as cited in Todres, 2005, p. 112) brings a focus to the analytical process, whereby the researcher's intent is to constantly seek precision and authenticity in reflecting the description of the phenomenon as experienced by the participants. We recognize the perceived difficulty in this descriptive approach from AOP, as seeking the essence of the lived experience, through an assumed accuracy of one's description of the experience, is premised on the foundation that an experience is solid and static, something that can be frozen in time and space. It also assumes that this analytical accuracy can be drawn across the same experience for several people to then describe the commonalities as the essence of the experience; thus the essence of an experience can be generalized. Doing so risks ignoring the multiplicities of a lived experience, and how the story of the experience can shift through each retelling of an experience for each individual, similar to what is acknowledged in narrative research (Ollerenshaw & Creswell, 2002). It also risks ignoring the more unique aspects of a lived experience, in seeking the commonality of that experience across all research participants. We discuss this latter point in our next section regarding tensions, but here we suggest one approach to offset this risk. Perhaps researchers can bridge this gap between phenomenology's assumption about being able to describe the essence of an experience for even one participant by acknowledging how meaning making itself is contextualized and fluid, for both participant and researcher, in the research process (Polkinghorne, 2005).

In interpretive phenomenology, perhaps the analysis is less challenging, given the openness to the researcher being more involved in the data collection and analysis process, under the guise of co-creating the knowledge. Crist and Tanner (2003) proffer that a systematic process enhances rigour, but also need not be linear, which thus limits the potential risk of over-interpretation by the researcher through a rigid process. They suggest an iterative process, a form of almost constant member-checking, wherein the researcher shifts back and forth between data collection and data analysis, seeking participant input throughout the process, while also using the notion of exemplar in creating a composite of the shared meaning of the experience. In this way, the analytical focus is on both the shared meaning between participants and the shared meaning between participants and the researcher. As such, we suggest a stronger fit with an AOP approach, where the power of the researcher is balanced against that of the participants (Rogers, 2012).

Above, we have discussed our understandings of phenomenological inquiry, with a particular focus on how AOP may intersect with both the descriptive and interpretive approach to phenomenology. However, there remain areas of tension that we continue to question below, recognizing the value in such forms of inquiry toward the social justice ends of AOP research.

REMAINING TENSIONS BETWEEN PHENOMENOLOGICAL INQUIRY AND AOP

We have considered how to interconnect AOP and phenomenology, but many tensions remain in bridging this approach to knowledge. Here we identify and discuss these tensions; we offer recommendations for managing these tensions and questions about where those tensions may remain, hoping we can further open the dialogue for exploration about bridging an AOP framework with phenomenological inquiry.

One of the difficulties in many current practices of phenomenological research is a conflation of both descriptive and interpretive approaches (Giorgi, 2008; Lopez & Willis, 2004). Given the philosophical distinctions between these two approaches, one risks questioning the credibility of the research, wherein the "methodological congruence" of the research becomes less clear (Creswell, 2013, p. 50). Qualitative research is often scrutinized for its lack of systematic process and rigour despite its valuable contributions, especially within social work research. Further, the philosophical and methodological foundations of descriptive and interpretive phenomenology will produce different research studies, yielding distinct conclusions, as demonstrated by the positionality of the researcher's knowledge and the essence of the phenomenon. Mixing different approaches to research is something we can expect in AOP-informed research (Fawcett & Hearn, 2004), but we must balance that with respecting the distinction between these two approaches and the general understanding of phenomenology. In the various elements of the research process, it is critical to avoid "method/methodological slurring" (May, 1991, as cited in Wimpenny & Gass, 2000, p. 1486). Doing so may seem antithetical to AOP, considering the broad range of theoretical foundations that inform AOP (Baines, 2011a). Why might we accept the multi-philosophical groundings of AOP, but then seek rigidity in the research process?

The fluidity of theory has been noted as a concern with respect to the fidelity of AOP as a framework to inform social work practice in any form (Sakamoto & Pitner, 2005), including research. The current blurring of philosophical differences in AOP, while a strength of AOP as an evolving theory, also requires more clearly delineated theoretical concepts in research as a way to counter the non-theoretical critique. Englander (2012) particularly addresses the issue of theoretical clarity throughout the research process in phenomenological inquiry "as part of a single, unified process with the same underlying theory" (p. 15) of science. Closely following the philosophical differences between descriptive and interpretive phenomenology is one way to approach this concern. Applying AOP as the underlying theoretical framework and clearly employing the distinct philosophical considerations of interpretive and descriptive phenomenology may silence questions of rigour and enhance the research as a contribution to emancipatory social justice.

Another tension is the concept of bracketing in phenomenology and the relationship between the researcher and the research topic. Descriptive phenomenology assumes the researcher can suspend their biases, assumptions, and previous experiences through bracketing, in order to focus on the phenomenon being studied (Gearing, 2004). Arguably, it is impossible to simply suspend one's history and life experience, even though it is assumed that the researcher contains, but also later acknowledges, their position and relation to the phenomenon (Laverty, 2003; Tufford & Newman, 2012). It has been suggested that this may be accomplished by keeping field notes where the researcher records their feelings or thoughts during the research process (Ortlipp, 2008; Wojnar & Swanson, 2007), and then unbrackets, whereby the researcher incorporates the bracketed text back into the research as a way of reconciling tensions of the researcher (Gearing, 2004). This notion seems contradictory to AOP's recognition of the constant influence of the researcher throughout the research process (Strier, 2007), and thus we question how authentic descriptive phenomenology may be within AOP research.

We acknowledge that bracketing sometimes is applied in interpretive phenomenology since descriptive and interpretive approaches often are conflated. However, in its purest sense, interpretive phenomenology does not employ bracketing and contests the notion itself (Reiners, 2012); the researcher co-creates the story through the interpretive process, such that the position of the researcher is included throughout the research process. However, the notion of the researcher co-creating the narrative requires intense reflection on the researcher's subject positioning and power. Given the tension we see between AOP-informed research and the commonness of bracketing in all forms of phenomenological inquiry (but especially in the descriptive approach), we wonder if the self-reflexive processes of AOP research may be a way to manage this tension. We also raise an additional question with respect to bracketing:

Even if we, as researchers, can bracket our own viewpoints, what of the participants? Does the fact that participants do not bracket their own preconceived notions in the telling of experience mean that our knowledge is based on a flawed understanding, already skewed from the things themselves (LeVasseur, 2003)?

Perhaps the current understanding of bracketing needs to be challenged more fully—is it a less visible form of power distinction between the researcher and participants, somehow suggesting the researcher has special knowledge and skills to be able to bracket in ways that it is assumed participants cannot? As a potential trace of positivism in qualitative research and specifically AOP-informed phenomenology, we suggest this is an area for further exploration, particularly in consideration of how power plays out in this assumption of researcher expertise (Rogers, 2012).

Building on our earlier point regarding methodological congruence, we raise the question here about the potential of "mixed discourse" (Giorgi, 1994, p. 192) in AOP-informed phenomenological inquiry. While this concept is applied to the importance of avoiding a blending of descriptive and interpretive phenomenology, we suggest that the same concept should be attended to with respect to another aspect of phenomenological inquiry: keeping the research focus specific to phenomenology's intent. We suggest that, given the limited use of phenomenological inquiry in social work research and the misnaming of some research as phenomenology, there seems to be a tendency of slipping into other elements of the phenomenon, such as seeking explanation. In effect, moving outside the limits of asking "how" and "what," when a researcher begins to ask "who" and "when," or "why," there is a risk of mixing phenomenology with narrative research or grounded theory research, respectively. We recognize that rigidity around the boundaries of research methods does not complement AOP research (Potts & Brown, 2005; Strier, 2007). While, in time, this may be appropriate as a reconstituted form of mixed-methods research (Mayoh & Onwuegbuzie, 2015), we ask here: Is social work sufficiently informed and rigorous within phenomenological inquiry at this point to begin reconstructing this approach to research?

Another tension between AOP and phenomenology rests with the practice of exposing the essence of the lived experience. How does one comprehend the essence of lived experience? How does a researcher analyze narratives in a phenome-nological research study? Building from the work of previous discussions of phenomenological research, Holloway and Todres (2005) offer five concepts as a foundation to the data analysis process, focused on shifting back and forth between the whole versus the individual experience, and thus also between the distinct meanings of the experience and the connections between those meanings. In this way, researchers such as Holloway and Todres (2005) suggest that the essence of the experience will emerge. However, we question this approach as one of reductionism, whereby unique elements of the lived experience of that phenomenon will become lost in the search for commonality. The reduction of lived experiences to an amalgamated whole is contrary to AOP's valuing of fluidity and multiplicity (Moosa-Mitha, 2005). Although some instances of commonality in lived histories can be anticipated, such as racism or homophobia, the intersections of identity complicate these commonalities. We especially anticipate this issue being problematic in interpretive phenomenology, where meaning making is fundamental to the interpretive process. And so we ask how might the phenomenological exercise of seeking an understanding of the essence of the lived experience be expanded to more fully reflect the experience, including those elements that are unique to any one individual? An AOP researcher may look to draw overarching conclusions based on systemic oppressions, while acknowledging the distinct experience of the individual.

Our final point regarding tensions between phenomenology and AOP focuses on the outcome of the research process. While we agree with Potts and Brown (2005) that the research process itself can be an effective experience to foster social change, they and Strier (2007) also note the importance of the research outcome as a mechanism or catalyst for social change. Yet this outward intention toward transformative purposes of research is not a commonly framed expectation in phenomenological inquiry. Instead, the focus is rooted in seeking knowledge to understand a phenomenon. While we recognize the importance of understanding the lived experience, we question here how phenomenology, in its "truest" sense, can be expanded toward a social change purpose. Perhaps since AOP is concerned with challenging systemic injustice, both descriptive and interpretive phenomenology offer a unique opportunity to illuminate oppression at a systemic level while contextualizing it within the individual's lived history.

This exploration of tensions in the intersection between phenomenological inquiry and AOP simply begins the dialogue. It is our intention that the issues we have raised here and the questions we have asked will engage others in the debate. In this way, our hope is to expand the possibilities for anti-oppressive research by drawing on the rich potential we see in phenomenology.

CONCLUSION

In this chapter, we have unpacked phenomenological inquiry to explore its potentialities for social work research, especially as an approach to social inquiry informed by anti-oppressive perspectives. Our own experiences with phenomenological research spurred us on this journey, to inform our future practice as researchers and to share our explorations. In doing so, we have sought to balance a space between the need for methodological clarity and fidelity for rigorous phenomenological inquiry and our own commitment to practising research within an AOP framework. To this end, we have explicated particular elements of two common approaches to phenomenology—descriptive and interpretive— and explored where these approaches potentially converge and diverge with anti- oppression practice. In discussing the tensions we have experienced, we challenge social work researchers to further engage with phenomenological inquiry from a critical standpoint toward transformation and social change.

9 | Unpacking Liminal Identity

Lessons Learned from a Life on the Margins

May Friedman, Associate Professor, School of Social Work, Ryerson University

WHO AM I?

There are things that I know.

I know myself as a mother, a daughter, and a partner. I know that I am a reader and a writer, a teacher, and a helper. I know that I am stubborn, that I laugh a lot and weep easily. I know myself as a singer and a baker; a friend; a lover of chocolate, reality TV, and disco.

Yet there are essential things I don't know. There are aspects of myself that defy easy categorization, that require endless hyphens and paragraphs of explanation. These ambiguous spaces have caused me uneasiness and discomfort, and often create discomfort in the people around me. For example: I can't fill out a census form without many minutes of contemplation. Attending the gay pride parade requires fervent introspection. Understanding myself through the lens of class is a complex algorithm of income versus upbringing divided by ethnicity and multiplied by migration.

In this chapter, I seek to interrogate the margins of my own identities and the fluidity with which my own travels—both literal and figurative—have indicated the limitations of coherent identity markers, specifically around the twin axes of race and ethnicity. In doing so, I aim to explore the role of autoethnography in social work research. By exploring my own experiences, I aim to expand my understanding of anti-oppression and to provide an analysis that uses my life as a starting point to larger critiques of identity politics and paths to activism. Beginning with an articulation of the ambiguity of my personal experiences with race and delving into the complications of a hybridized and intersected ethnic identity, I aim to expose the benefits of liminality and the ways that embodied intersections may provide an important site of analysis and discussion.

ON AUTOETHNOGRAPHY

I have learned best from stories. I have always devoured novels and memoirs; my academic path meandered through English literature, delved into memoir and autobiography, and then to social work counselling toward research on blogs and personal writing. The thread that has blended all my scholarly pursuits has always been a focus on storytelling as a means of acquiring knowledge. As a parent, I tell my children stories—other stories, those written in books, but also their own stories, the stories of their births and babyhoods, narratives that make sense of their selves and their places in the world. Likewise, as an educator, I encourage my students to be ruthlessly self-reflexive, to interrogate their own histories as a sense-making venture. It is thus a natural extension for me to use autoethnography as a means of exploring systems and structures, and contributing to a dialogue about identity, community, and activism. Autoethnography takes up the life as source of research knowledge and allows for grappling with "politically and personally problematic worlds of everyday life" (Denzin, 2003a, p. 236). Used in a politically authentic context, autoethnography can be transgressive, an example of "research as resistance" (Brown & Strega, 2005).

Autoethnography is full of what Massaquoi (2011) calls "transformative disruptions," moments of discomfort and disquiet that provide hidden wisdom or access to complicated truths. I want to use autoethnography to consider some of the transformative disruptions I have encountered in my life as someone with an intersected and not easily categorized identity. I aim to use this autoethnographic moment to consider some of the specific blurry boundaries of race and ethnicity that exist "outside belonging" (Probyn, 1996). If, as Kimpson (2005) suggests, "critical autobiographical narratives themselves transgress academic and disciplinary expectations about how research is 'supposed' to be conducted" (p. 73), I want to use this space as a further transgression of those neat census boxes, of the lines of black and white.

BEGINNING WITH THE BODY: ON RACE

I am a brown woman with very curly hair. I have been read, variously, as white, biracial, and Black. I have also been seen as "Middle Eastern," "Mediterranean," "ethnic," "exotic," and "soooo interesting!" My fat, brown self has interesting chameleon properties—people try to engage me speaking Greek, Armenian, Arabic, Farsi, Italian, and Spanish, plus many other languages that I either can't remember or couldn't recognize. While my race and ethnicity have always been ambiguous, I cannot remember a time that I didn't feel like a conversation piece. Often my shade is determined by my context, where I'm assumed to be like the people around me; at other times, the discrepancy between me and those around causes more tension. For example, the confusion about my phenotype is often curiously muted when I am out with my brown father or my little brown son—"Ah! We can place you in a set!"; heightened when I walk around Toronto with my lighter-skinned children or my fair partner—"Is that your real hair?" "Are they *your* children?" Likewise, a shift in geography portends a shift in status: Living in Ottawa, my race is publicly discussed more often than in Toronto; on a trip to Atlantic Canada, I am constantly questioned. In Israel, visiting my huge family, I am simultaneously, unambiguously racialized, and curiously, unexpectedly, welcomed. When I am working as a social worker in a busy and ethnically diverse community health centre, clients are constantly asking about my origins, perhaps in response to the power that allows me to ask endless questions of them. "Where are you from? No, where are you *really* from?" Years later, I am still unsure how to answer.

There are many people who fall into ambiguous ethnic categories, bifurcated and hyphenated identities; in Victor Turner's (1967) usage, we are "threshold people who elude or slip through the network of classifications that normally locate states and positions in cultural spaces" (p. 95). I understand that my experience is not unique, and in fact feel a delicious kinship with others whom I have encountered who are read ambiguously. I have recently begun participating in a feminist group that we have titled "The Paint Chip," because we are all somewhere on the vague continuum that traditional analyses of race, the fixed tick boxes that measure us, cannot contain. At the same time, I recognize, both through the racism I have experienced and that I see around me, the entrenched reality of race and racism as a powerful organizing category, even as I contend that my own body destabilizes race as transcendent. I offer here an analysis of my own experience as not only someone who is read ambiguously, but as someone who cannot accurately or consistently narrate my *own* experience of race. I aim to expose some of the lessons learned through these shifting identity markers by considering both how I am seen by others and how I have come to know myself.

E-RACED

As a child, I understood myself as white. My parents, despite much evidence and many experiences of racism to the contrary, would likely still argue that we are white. I grew up in racially diverse Toronto, in a neighbourhood with many families who were, like my family, Jewish. Yet they weren't like my family. We spoke Arabic and Hebrew, instead of English peppered with Yiddishisms. The intense collective memory of the Holocaust that informs the diasporic Jewish community was not the collective memory of my people. Both physically and culturally, I did not resemble the Jewish community around me, yet that was the only site of difference that I was offered to explain my lack of belonging in mainstream Canadian culture. bell hooks defines "homeplace" as "spaces, places, people, events, histories, practices, and care that offer respite and help people recuperate from a hostile normative world" (Schneider, 2013, p. 115). I understood my body and culture as non-normative, but the Jewish homeplace being put forth—by my parents and others—was likewise unfamiliar, a further site that emphasized my difference from within difference. As a young person, however, I did not have the capacity for critical reflection to understand my uneasiness with the discrepancies between the explanations I was offered and my experiences of embodying difference. I didn't know about internalized racism or generational trauma—I just knew that my parents said we were white, and that Jews were always white, weren't they? Why else would my relatives keep saying terrible things about Black people or displaying their obvious fear of anyone *they* viewed as non-white? In the face of this racism I felt—albeit unconsciously—that I certainly couldn't make alliances with Black folks; could not seek out places to learn to tame—or maybe even love—my curls; to learn to confront ugly stares. But I was the only "white" girl I knew with scalp burns from using chemicals to—badly—relax her Afro; the only Jewish person I knew outside my family who served pickled mango at family parties and watched the cousins ululate. I experienced the mocking comments made to my accented, brown parents and the intense scrutiny of—and humiliating comments about—my hair and body as shame. I didn't know we were racialized—I just thought we were personally, irredeemably wrong. My parents couldn't or wouldn't provide a homeplace, hoping that denial and hard work would somehow ameliorate their brown skin. Perhaps as a result, that shame continues into the present day. I feel it when I see the double-take when I reveal myself as a university professor or the confusion when I introduce myself as the mother of my children. While I have grown up to name these experiences as rooted in the ways I am seen as raced, I nonetheless experience them in my body as fear, discomfort, and shame.

Nonetheless, I still feel palpable discomfort in naming these experiences as racism. If my experiences make it clear that I'm not the mainstream Jewish kid I thought I was growing up, I am terrified that I have instead become the white girl who thinks she's badass for wearing a bindi and henna tattoos—metaphorically speaking. At the same time, there is a unique awfulness to growing up understanding myself as white yet nonetheless experiencing racism. My family maintained their somewhat fictional "whiteness," and its subsequent silencing of any discussion of race, despite all evidence to the contrary. This has been increasingly challenging, especially in the aftermath of 9/11 when Arab looks and language became much more focused objects of suspicion. As a result, I grew up in a marked body without any common experience or language to make sense of my experience. I was in my late 20s before I understood that the mean kids, the awkward public interactions, the fetishization of my looks could all be contained by the word *racism*. While I am not always read as racialized, I do not know when or where the privilege of whiteness will be offered. This has resulted in a heightened awareness of the world around me, but also a degree of suspicion and fear since I do not ever know what to expect.

It is important for me to, in the words of Haig-Brown (2009), decolonize this autobiography, to attempt to name the privileges of being ambiguously racialized as well as the complicated impact of immigration. My family was perceived as white enough for my father to be a "good" immigrant and thus achieve a measure of financial success despite his eighth-grade education. My father, who left Israel because of his extreme discomfort with the Zionist project of appropriating land, settled his family in Canada without a moment's unease over the provenance of his new "chosen land." He thus elected for participation in what Sa'ar (2005) terms "the liberal bargain," by which "some members of marginalized groups internalize liberal epistemology to maximize security and optimize their life options" (p. 681). I did not learn about Indigenous rights or struggles until graduate school. At the same time, I certainly did not understand myself as a natural Canadian, and in the absence of any "blood memory" (Baskin, 2006), I was bewildered by the ways I was taken up as I navigated the world around me. I wish that my discomfort came with a politicized understanding of colonialism, but it instead manifested in a vague uneasiness with how people looked at me and spoke to me, with the fact that people would pull my tight curls in fascination while I rode the streetcar, with the closed-lipped frown my dad would give when he handed over our passports at the border and announced his birthplace as "Iraq."

Whiteness is sometimes underestimated in discussions of race; Calafell (2013) argues that this may be especially so in autoethnography. While I have come to understand myself as racialized, I also can't ignore the times and places where I have been extended white privilege. If that privilege is inconsistently offered, however, it leaves me in a place where I am both racialized and not, both white and brown. My experiences are ambiguous, shifting. I am claimed by everyone. Friends who are not politicized—often, but not always white folks—are uncomfortable with me naming myself as racialized: "I-I-I just never think of you that way!" I speak with biracial people and other brown folks about our experiences as insiders and outsiders. And I am part of a minority that is explicitly understood in Israeli culture as Black, and have been understood as Black—rather than biracial or brown—by Black people in Canada. These experiences have confirmed for me that "describing how you enact important identities is an escaping analogy. Perhaps part of the problem is fixed spaces and identities" (Faulkner, 2013, p. 46). In order to unpack the potential of my ambiguous identity, I will aim to break free from those fixed spaces and explore the possibilities of an unfixed self as a means of opening up new conversations and understandings about race.

ON LIMINALITY

Turner (1967) suggests that liminal identities may offer "a realm of pure possibility, whence novel configurations of ideas and relations may arise" (p. 97). Observing the shifts in reactions to my physiology as I travel though the world—a short streetcar ride is enough to engender different responses—has allowed me to understand, viscerally, the limitations of race as an organizing marker. I am hyper-aware of spaces where I am read as an insider or outsider, and I have a mindfulness about social location that comes from having the dichotomy of privilege and oppression constantly exposed and denaturalized. Importantly, this understanding has not denuded my analysis of race as a critical marker in the lives of people of colour; rather, my uncertain categorization has led to a more conclusive understanding of the ways that people are treated differently on the basis of race, as I see the ways that I am treated differently based on how I am read. This embodied knowledge of liminality blends into my practice and teaching as a social worker. If "the purpose of praxis is to enact one's conscious knowledge and practical wisdom with the ethical and political intention of living well" (Green & Friedman, 2013, p. 7), I aim to take up the challenges presented by my bifurcated and ambiguous identity. I further take the knowledge gained from my unconsciencized upbringing and extend it to compassion for people around me who may likewise lack the tools to fully recognize the positive and negative implications of their social locations. Liminality may afford potential that can't be found in other theoretical sites, such as theories of intersectionality that may simply reify stable identities but consider them in relation to one another. By contrast, a liminal analysis may take up Lather's (1991) challenge that "remarks *toward* a definition be used to displace the desire to comprehend, to 'clearly understand'" (p. 5). In this effort to avoid "clear understanding," I can find radical possibilities on the margins of stable identity markers.

I take Boylorn's (2011) challenge that "being consciously self-reflexive also requires me to accept what I see and use that as a starting point" (p. 184). If my race cannot be clearly or consistently defined, then where do I belong? How do I negotiate the difficult terrain between insider and ally? At the same time, my ambiguous existence opens the door to considering the need for an analysis of race and ethnicity that responds to ambiguity and sees it as theoretically and practically fruitful. It is my ability to walk in between spaces that are meant to be understood as contained and demarcated that gives me insight into race as a social construction, and into the limits of strict identity categories as means of both categorization and activism. Somewhere between accompanying my father, named Aziz, to a doctor's appointment—brown!—and being in the world with my blue-eyed partner, named Friedman—white!—there is delicious possibility in unpacking what Turner (1967) sees as the threshold; what Anzaldúa (1987) considers the *mestiza* consciousness, the consciousness of the Borderlands.

Butler (1990) suggests that "if a stable notion of gender no longer proves to be the foundational premise of feminist politics, perhaps a new sort of feminist politics is now desirable to contest the very reification of gender and identity, one that will take the variable construction of identity as both a methodological and normative prerequisite, if not a political goal" (p. 9). If, like Anzaldúa (1987) and others, I cannot avoid the "variable construction of identity," I find deep resonance in theories that expose the ambiguity of identity as a source of political potential. At the same time, I worry about the limits of postmodern identity to harness effective change. On the one hand, even as I teach my students to be critical of the efficiencies of neoliberalism, I see that rapid political and social shifts have often been seated in coherent identity markers, civil rights brought about by identity politics, in what Butler calls the "reification of identity." On the other, I heed Keating (1998), who suggests that an "emphasis on mutually exclusive identities makes it impossible to recognize commonalities among differently situated social actors, thus preventing the establishment of effective alliances" (p. 36). In order to consider the limits of liminality, then, I must take a detour through my own politics of identity.

THE AMAZING DISAPPEARING, REAPPEARING ARAB: ON ETHNICITY

Okay, wait, what? Arab … and *Jewish*? *"White"*… AND *brown*? Where are you *really* from? There is a curiosity, perhaps understandable, extended toward those of us who are not easily contained by known identity boundaries: the woman with the Irish first name paired with a Sikh last name; the blue-eyed, brown-skinned child with the reddish Afro. While some of this fascination is undoubtedly its own form of racism, a means of further consuming difference, my engagement with other people's stories makes me feel a bit generous toward those who want to hear my own. Perhaps to get the full benefit of my liminal identity, it is important to unpack some of the details of my ethnicity.

Despite my situation on the Borderland of ethnicity, I am not, in fact, a mestiza, a mix of multiple ethnicities and histories. My parents belonged to a relatively large Jewish community in Iraq, where their families had lived for thousands of years. While Jewish Iraqis experienced periods of violence and anti-Semitism, they were in many ways well integrated into broader Iraqi society, with engagement in civic and cultural life (Rejwan, 2010). The rise of Zionism led to unrest for Jewish citizens of many Arab countries—whether or not they were allied with this movement. Beginning in 1930, Jewish Iraqis experienced significant persecution, and by 1948, there were major limits to their citizenship, including their expulsion from areas of education, employment, and commerce. In 1950, in response to the Arab–Israeli war, a law of one year's duration was passed allowing Jews to leave Iraq freely, in return for revoking their Iraqi citizenship. In response to this law, the nascent government of Israel organized airlifts of Jewish Iraqis—alongside many other Jews from Arab countries (Rejwan, 2004). My parents, along with 120,000 other Jews of Iraq, moved to Israel, where they met and married.

The official story that the Jewish community feeds me is about rescue of the poor, misbegotten Jews out of the hands of their Arab oppressors. The actual story, of course, is much more complicated. The land of Israel was created by the expulsion of poor, brown—Muslim and Christian—Arabs, and was then repopulated by poor, brown—

Jewish—Arabs (Lavie, 2012). Yet the simple explanation of colonialist expansion does not adequately contain my family's experiences, of living in refugee camps full of canvas tents for years, eventually replaced by cinderblock slums; of having nowhere else to be, no place to return to. The situation of Israel/Palestine, both then and now, is very, very complicated, and neither official story—Jewish land grab/Holocaust survivors make the desert bloom—adequately conveys my family's experiences. Without entering into the political fray and devolving into a full analysis of the Middle East, it is important for me to understand my here and now by considering the experiences of Jews from Arab lands in Israel.

Migration to Israel required a profound shift in identity for those of Arab-Jewish origin. Iraqi Jews, like other Jews from Arab countries, went from being a religious minority but ethnic majority to suddenly belonging to a religious and political majority that instead defined them on the basis of race. Ella Shohat (2006) writes that "if in the Arab world, prior to their 'Exodus,' their Jewishness was subjected to surveillance, in Israel their affiliation with an Arab cultural geography was similarly disciplined and punished" (p. 335). To avoid this cultural marking, many Arab-Jewish arrivals attempted to "Zionize" as successfully as possible. Thus, my mother went from "Samira"—her birth name—to "Shulamit"; my father, though still legally "Aziz," is known in Israel as "Uzi." Similarly, as a community, Jews from Arab lands defy easy labelling, suggesting "a terminological crisis in which no single term seems to fully represent a coherent identity" (Shohat, 2006, p. 334). The term currently enjoying the greatest popularity for Jewish Israelis of Arab origin is *Mizrachim*—literally "Eastern" or "Oriental" Jews. Smadar Lavie (2011) suggests that "most Mizrachim vehemently reject the identity descriptor 'Arab Jews'" (p. 57), suggesting that the attempt to distance themselves from Arabness, seen as so antithetical to Jewish identity in the popular imaginary, is a defining identity marker. Lavie further remarks that "in the past, the mainstream forced Mizrachim to shed Arab markers because the Ashkenazi regime conceived their Arabness as dangerously primitive. These days, Mizrachim who make it into the mainstream self-censor the discrimination and humiliation they have encountered to become 'brown-skinned gringos'" (Lavie, 2012, p. 782). Yet Arabness is not so easily shed.

The ruling elite in Israel, both in the past and present, is composed of Jews of Eastern European—Ashkenazi—origin. Despite the fact that in the present day non-European Israeli Jews make up half of the population of Israel (Lavie, 2011) and almost two-thirds of the Jewish population (Lavie, 2012), "Mizrachim constitute the majority of Israel's disenfranchised" (Lavie, 2011, p. 300; see also Sa'ar, 2005). Lavie (2012), writing about her experiences as a Yemeni Israeli insider/outsider, states, "A split second is all an Israeli needs to racially typecast me. My phenotype almost always trumps my privilege" (p. 780). Shohat (2006) suggests that if correlations may be made between Palestinians and North American First Nations—as Indigenous Peoples—there are likewise correlations between the situation of African-American and Canadian people and Mizrachi Israelis—as racialized but non-Indigenous peoples. Shohat (2006) articulates the ways that many Mizrachi Israelis understood themselves as clearly "other" with respect to race, as can be seen in the rise of the Mizrachi "Black Panther" movement of the 1970s, which drew its name from the American movement of the same name.

In 1992, Lavie set out to interview "border poets," men and women whose identities were not easily subsumed into the project of Israeli nationalism and Jewish culture. In Lavie's interview with prominent Israeli poet Amira Hess, Hess suggests that in an effort to avoid the ghettoization of being an "ethnic" artist, she has attempted, ineffectively, to "pass" in Israeli society:

> I was thinking, what's a Mizrachi woman? Nothing. Maybe I always dreamed of being white, but kept killing the white woman in me. Now the white woman is dead, because I'm aware of who I am. When I wanted to be white, I managed to be white in the world, but was still black under my skin. Now I know I could never have been white in the world, because black is more than my color. It's my essence. My thinking. My feelings. It's my history of home in Iraq. … [Passing] was a matter of everyday survival in Israel. You know, they passed on so much Auschwitz gas to us. (Lavie, 1995, p. 413)

I shiver reading these words, consider the "Auschwitz gas" I have myself taken in. Yet my experiences are not the same as those of my Mizrachi cousins still residing in Israel. My experience of racism in a North American context is more subtle, more convoluted. Neither "Jewish" nor "Arab" adequately contain my ethnicity or background. The history of my family's migration means that labelling myself as Arab, the literal truth, is unavailable. In North America, where the Jewish experience is often understood as unilaterally Ashkenazi—with limited room for "Sephardi," or Spanish/Moroccan/Algerian Judaism—labelling myself as Jewish is equally fraught. North American Jews are rarely familiar with Mizrachi identity; non-Jewish people are almost never aware of the capacity for Arab and Jewish history to simultaneously inhabit the same body. Ella Shohat (2003) writes:

> I recall a well established colleague who despite my elaborate lessons on the history of Arab Jews, still had trouble understanding that I was not a tragic anomaly—for instance, the daughter of an Arab (Palestinian) and an Israeli (European Jew). Living in North America makes it even more difficult to communicate that we are Jews and yet entitled to our Middle Eastern difference. And that we are Arabs and yet entitled to our religious difference, like Arab Christians and Arab Muslims. To be a European or American Jew has hardly been perceived as a contradiction, but to be an Arab Jew has been seen as a kind of logical paradox, even an ontological subversion. (para. 6)

In addition to a lack of familiarity with the specifics of Arab Jewry, the dominant North American Jewish community is invested in maintaining the story of Israel as a promised land; Israeli atrocities toward Palestinians are wrapped in justifications and any discussion of internal racism between Israeli Jews is silenced. I am thus both protected by my Jewish identity and set up as a conundrum, a riddle to be solved. I am suddenly neither/both Jewish and Arab. In Canada, my father reverts to Aziz; my sister, named after my aunt Aziza who became "Yehudit"—literally Jewess—in Israel, becomes Judy; marked by the challenges of living in Israel in Arab bodies, my parents reinvent themselves as good "white" Canadian immigrants. At the same time, when I visit Israel and travel with a group of North American Jews, our Mizrachi bus driver sees that I don't fit in, I am not a "normal" diasporic visitor, and calls me "Ha Iraqit Sheli"—my Iraqi girl.

Shohat (2006) suggests that the ambiguity of the North American Arab-Jewish identity opens possibilities: "while one might rightly argue that there is no single Mizrachi history, the term highlights the dislocation and the shaping of a new hybrid identity, neither simply 'Arab' nor simply 'Jewish'" (p. 336). Perhaps I am "from" this new hybrid space, a queered Borderland of liminality? Perhaps my body and my history take up Shohat's (2006) challenge that "genders, sexualities, races, classes, nations, and even continents exist not as hermetically sealed entities but, rather as part of a permeable interwoven relationality?" (p. 2). Yet, in the context of activism and social work, this permeability can sometimes be viewed as suspect, as a threat to the coherence of identity that is required to make change.

ACTIVISM, IDENTITY, AND INTERSECTIONS

Why do I *need* to determine which box contains my ethnicity? Why does it matter whether or not I am understood as racialized? Writing in *Black, White and Jewish*, Rebecca Walker (2001) relishes spaces of instability:

> I am more comfortable in airports than I am in either of the houses I call, with undeserved nostalgia, Home. Airports are limbo spaces—blank, undemanding, neutral. Expectations are clear. I am the passenger. I am coming or going. I am late, on time, or early. I must have a ticket. I must have identification. I must not carry a weapon. Beyond these qualifications, I do not have to define this body. I do not have to belong to one camp, school, or race, one fixed set of qualifiers, adjectives based on someone else's experience. I do not have to remember who I, or anyone else, thinks I am. (p. 4)

Like Walker (2001), I relish spaces that allow me to remain undefined. I contest her supposition, however, that airports are neutral and undemanding spaces for racialized people. At the airport, I am most mindful of my Arab body; marked in part by the race of my travelling companions, I may be read as more or less white, but ultimately am more likely to be pulled out of line, to have my bag rudely unpacked, to have my shoes X-rayed, than others around me. I explicitly fear airports as sites where my body speaks more loudly than my Canadian passport or my over-education. Faulkner (2013) suggests that "identity labels are political by necessity, even as experiences swim—drown?—in the Sea of Flux" (p. 42). While liminality opens possibilities, it does not teach me how to orient—ha!—my little brown son to a different way of life than his whiter siblings. It doesn't help me navigate the feeling of being a stranger (Ahmed, 2012) in my professional life, of the lack of safety I often feel in the world. While liminality may provide opportunities to destabilize race and ethnicity, to render explicit the limits of identities as social constructs, it doesn't necessarily provide much guidance on how to navigate the spaces where I'm understood as racialized, Jewish, Arab, or, for that matter, white.

There are further problems. I believe in activism and aim to harness the world's transformative potential. Yet my inability to categorize my life and my body have made this activist stance quite difficult. With whom do I march? For whom do I advocate? Borrowing from disability activists who maintain "nothing about us without us!", how do I proceed if I can't count myself among an "us"? In Israel I might, like my beautiful cousins, join the burgeoning Mizrachi feminist movement and find my place as a feminist of colour decrying the intersection of racism and sexism (Lavie, 2011, 2012; Sa'ar, 2005). In Canada, there is no Mizrachi feminist movement and joining with other feminists of colour has been an uneasy process. I am mindful of Alcoff's claim that "how what is said gets heard depends on who says it" (as quoted in Calafell, 2013, p. 10), which makes me very wary of how my body is read and, thus, how my voice is heard. Will I be understood as a white woman commandeering spaces of colour? An ally? An insider? My self-identity is characterized most by creeping uncertainty. Like Martha Kuwee Kumsa (2011), I have learned about "the bitter way that identities are multiple and fluid" (p. 238). I knew so little about myself until relatively recently, and am still being blown away by my discoveries about both Mizrachi identity generally and my embodied experiences specifically; this uncertainty makes it difficult to meet other people's uncertainty about me with conviction. As a result, I find myself sometimes reluctant to participate in formal activist spaces because they may begin from an insistence on formal identity politics. This may be especially true in sites of anti-oppressive social work that, in well-intentioned attempts to respond to oppression, may unwittingly reify identity categories. Kumsa (2011) writes that,

> Essentialist [anti-oppressive practice] starts from the fundamental assumptions that societies are riddled with conflict and our mundane practices are embedded in unequal relations of power. Often, however, these conflicts are restricted to those *between*

"mainstream" and "minority" communities, whereas within groups solidarity is emphasized, thus creating homogeneous categories and false binaries—that is, false unity within a group and false opposition between groups. (p. 238)

Inhabiting a body that explodes the binaries of white and Black, of Jew and Arab, can render me a threat to the homogeneity of identity-based organizing. As a result, I may find my experiences erased or downplayed by others who have experienced oppression. While I feel compassion for anyone who has suffered, the erasure of my life, of my history, in favour of racial and cultural cohesion, feels like its own form of violence. Stuart argues that,

The problem was not, in a strange way, that we took the implications of organizing around identity too far, but that we didn't take it far enough. Had we really pushed this debate far enough, we would have come to appreciate that we are all oppressor and oppressed. … Instead of appreciating the interconnectedness of our oppressions we all saw our interests as mutually antagonistic, instead of making alliances we were in competition with one another. (as quoted in Keating, 1998, p. 36)

In response to my own feelings, which echo Stuart's concerns, I have instead been drawn to non-traditional activist spaces such as online community building that celebrates a diversity of identities, strategies, and tactics and may resist the myths and methods of totalizing identities "in favour of a convoluted and fractured chorus of responses and connections" (Friedman, 2013, p. 153).

CONCLUSION

When I need to reveal myself for official purposes, I am sometimes confounded by the list of possibilities—Black? White? West Asian? North African?—and, thus, often resort to the box marked "Other." This box generally has a space for an explanation underneath. This chapter is my convoluted explanation for selecting the "Other" box, an attempt to trap the shifting and uncertain markers of my body and history, and to reveal both the inadequacy of my labels and the truths I find between them.

The lessons from the edges of identity may be as difficult to trap as the identities themselves. I want to tie my ideas up into a neat knot and carefully present an itemized list of conclusions that stem from my experiences. King (2003) states that "the truth about stories is that that's all we are" (p. 2). If I am the sum total of my stories, it is tempting to make those stories conclusive; yet it is precisely my inability to easily categorize, or neatly delineate, the details of my life that results in an incapacity to narrate a complete and coherent ending. I find comfort in both autoethnography and theories of hybridity and liminality, in places that have room to welcome disruption and view unstable terrain as theoretical and practically fruitful.

Taking up this form of research feels dangerous and very vulnerable; it is tempting to retreat to the position of arm's-length researcher looking at others, instead of looking inward. I am reminded of Jones's (2010) charge that "reflexivity has got to hurt. Reflexivity is laborious" (p. 124). It is precisely this reflexivity, and this discomfort, that is essential in anti-oppressive social work research and practice. Such reflexivity charges us with the responsibility of inhabiting our oppressions and our privileges and the uneasy ambiguities between. For true anti-oppression practice and research to take place, we must embrace uncertainty, both in terms of understanding societies and in terms of looking within ourselves. Kumsa (2011) reminds us that

> it is very easy, very seductive, to dig in and retreat to the position of not taking it personally, to believe that it is 'their' problem, not yours. I hope AOP practitioners drop out of that 'race to innocence' and instead pursue the more difficult transformative route of challenging themselves and considering whether they inhabit an oppressive dimension of social relations. (p. 245)

Such a challenge will require social work researchers and practitioners to move beyond stale analyses of identity that reify and entrench categorization. A consideration of identity as fluid, malleable, and unstable does not undermine the social relations that make racism, homophobia, and other oppressions very real for the bodies who experience them. Rather, however, such an analysis would allow social workers to dig into a true engagement with individuals and communities that see the uncertainly situated markers of virtually all lives. Rather than memorizing the rota of oppressed and privileged bodies, truly anti-oppressive practitioners must see identity as dynamic, both self- and other-determined, and brilliantly interactive with social, familial, and environmental contexts. This is true in terms of the engagement of AOP practitioners looking outward, but it is also essential in terms of self-reflexive practice.

Plump and Geist-Martin (2013) assert that "the feeling of being betwixt and between our multiple identities is a critical component of being successful in the work we do in our ethnographic research" (p. 61). I want to push even further, to suggest that the inability to easily inhabit our identities themselves, and not just their multiplicity, may provide unique theoretical perspectives and suggestions. There are opportunities here for supple and permeable alliances and actions that, while potentially less efficient than traditional models of identity politics, may result in a less divisive and more robust path toward social transformation.

10 | Decolonizing a Graduate Research Course … Moving Away from Innocence and Ignorance

Susan Silver, Associate Professor, School of Social Work, Ryerson University

THE INCIDENT

September 2007 was an exciting new academic semester, as our new MSW program was beginning and I would be teaching the required research course called Advanced Research for Social Change. Our MSW program is quite distinct in that it positions anti-oppression as the sole focus of study. Hoping to capture this focus, I framed the course in a manner that would critically expose and challenge the domination and marginalization produced and reproduced in the research process. This would require exposing the taken-for-granted and normalized practices that construct research as a neutral problem-solving process. Instead, I was positioning social work research as a process and a product, as a site of struggle and resistance, and as a powerful strategy for transformative change (Brown & Strega, 2005). I selected critical readings, many of which are drawn from the course textbook (Brown & Strega, 2005) and explicitly cited in this narrative, that would allow me to develop and locate this course within anti-oppression practice. The central epistemological questions that I used to frame the course included:

- What counts as legitimate knowledge?
- What are the processes of knowledge production?
- Which methodologies are privileged and claim to yield the "truth"?
- Which methodologies are marginalized/trivialized?
- Who is entitled to engage in these processes?
- Whose interests are being served?

In addition to these epistemological concerns, I sought to expose students to the various methodological frameworks, debates, tensions, and movements within social work research. I dutifully incorporated every framework and method, including critical discursive analysis, evidence-based practice, evaluation research, critical ethnography, Indigenous methodologies, and participatory action research. I further designed assignments that would allow students to work with research methods to critically examine how these methods are situated within and across research frameworks. This was all to be accomplished in this one-semester course. The new syllabus was reviewed by my colleagues; everyone was very excited by how I was positioning this required course in our new graduate program.

And so with much anticipation, the first class commenced and proceeded quite smoothly. The typical fear and anxiety about research surfaced, as did some concern that research would take up such a large space in the graduate program. In my experiences teaching undergraduate research, social work students seem to have a very tentative relationship with research. Perhaps this anxiety results from research courses being more technical in contrast to the reflective approach taken in the social work practice courses. As we reviewed the syllabus and began talking about repositioning research within anti-oppression practice, I detected a small degree of excitement and perhaps even a sense of relief that this research course would be different!

In the second class, we began to form groups for the "methods" presentations. There were 30 students in the class, and I conveniently came up with a list of 10 research methods: case study, critical discourse analysis, experimental group and single system designs, focus groups, historical research, individual interviews, surveys, secondary analysis, and participant observation. As I listed the methods, I was asked why the sharing circle wasn't included as one of the methods. I thought about the question for less than a minute. I then responded by saying that a sharing circle was very much like a focus group, and so whichever group was assigned the focus group method could also discuss the sharing circle, demonstrating its similarities and differences with the focus group. This response was not challenged at that time. As the semester unfolded, an indescribable but palpable tension seemed ever-present. I attributed some of the tension to the typical mid-semester anxiety, never implicating myself in this context. So, much to my surprise, I was called out during the presentations and accused of what Linda Tuhiwai Smith (2012) refers to as "epistemic violence," an act of colonialism in which I, a white academic, used my Western lens to marginalize Aboriginal ways of knowing by positioning the sharing circle in the category of a focus group.

I sat there, shaken to my core, emotionally overwhelmed, in total disbelief, wanting to run away and never face this class again, but knowing that I would have to be back the next week. This event became a very critical incident, in that it affected me profoundly and marked a significant turning point in my thinking (Fook, 2012).

I have selected critical autoethnography, a form of critical ethnographic writing, through which to share my reflective process with readers. As described by Ellis and Bochner (2000),

> The stories we write put us into conversation with ourselves, we expose our vulnerabilities, conflicts, choices and values. We take measure of our uncertainties,

our mixed emotions and the multiple layers of our experience. Our accounts seek to express the complexities and difficulties of coping and feeling resolved, showing how we changed over time as we struggled to make sense of our experiences. Often our accounts are unflattering and imperfect, but human and believable. (p. 748)

My story is one of attempting to create meaning of this turning point in my life.

HOW COULD I ...

How could I have reproduced the very marginalization and domination that we were trying to expose in this research course? I left that classroom in utter anguish and spent the next week in critical reflection and angst. How could I have excluded the sharing circle as a research method in the first place, and then summarily positioned it in the focus group category? This became even more troubling as I had intended on covering Indigenous methodologies in a later class.

These two acts of epistemic violence had the power to unsettle the very subject positions that I invest in. I have always considered myself an ally, a researcher committed to participatory approaches, putting students first—or as Heron (2005) and Todd (2011) describe it, being the good white subject. Confronted with the unsettling knowledge that I didn't "get it right" (Heron, 2005, p. 349), do I race to innocence (Fellows & Razack, 1998) or do I claim ignorance (Tuana, 2006) to deny my complicity in perpetuating colonialism? I have come to realize that, however unintentionally, I did both.

My struggle during that first week was probably more visceral and emotional than it was cognitive. Perhaps this response could be expected given the powerful and dramatic manner in which the charge was made. I sought guidance and comfort from colleagues that I felt "knew" me and could attest to the very subjectivities that had been called into question. As it got closer to my inevitable reappearance in the class, I began to re-engage with the course readings on Indigenous methodologies, including Baskin (2005a), Lavallée (2009), Smith (2012), and Kovach (2005). I began to focus on the "sacred meaning" that sharing circles have in Indigenous cultures, and it is this sacredness that distinguishes them from the Western-ness of the focus group (Lavallée, 2009, p. 29). So while the focus group methodology has its roots in Western corporate marketing that fuels consumer capitalism (Comor, 2008), sharing circles, in stark contrast, are grounded in traditional Aboriginal Peoples' epistemologies, cultural protocols, and values (Baskin, 2005a).

Baskin (2005a) describes the sharing circle as a storytelling methodology in which "participants join together, sit in a circle, incorporate spirituality through smudging, prayer, and the presence of sacred objects, follow cultural protocols of sharing food and gifts, and engage in a research process that involves the telling of their stories" (para. 2). It is a place of comfort, but the sharing circle also recognizes the importance of making space for healing, as "there is much pain woven into our stories" (para. 15).

As I read and re-read these passages, the spirituality of the sharing circle took on a profoundness that I had not felt before. In trying to understanding the spiritual essence of the sharing circle, I began reaching into my own Jewish culture, looking for sacred spiritual spaces that are of significance to me. It was then that I invoked the Sabbath candle-lighting ceremony, an integral part of my Jewish culture. I recalled the powerful images of my mother lighting the Sabbath candles, waiting for the flames to glow, gathering the smoke with her outstretched arms, praying for her family, and quietly crying as she remembered and mourned those that she had lost. It is in these sacred spaces, reached through our spiritual and cultural practices, that our past, our present, and our future co-exist. In that moment, by connecting with my own Jewish culture I could appreciate the significance of the sharing circle and how my Western classification of it had violated this sacredness. What I could not understand from my Western research lens, I was now able to begin to appreciate by leaning on my own spiritual space. This story of spiritual recognition is the story that I shared with the students during that next class. This moment also marked the beginning of my new journey to decolonize the research course.

When I reflect back on those moments, I am left with some unsettling thoughts. I can't help but wonder whether invoking my Jewish identity constituted a "race to innocence" (Fellows & Razack, 1998). The candle-lighting ceremony, as performed by my mother, signifies many aspects of my culture, but also the recognition of a history that is replete with pain and oppression. Did I inadvertently use my Jewish identity and its minority status to mitigate my "whiteness" (Yee, this volume) and secure a place on the margin (Fellows & Razack, 1998)? Fellows and Razack (1998) talk of "competing marginalities," in which those "challenged about their domination respond by calling attention to their own subordination" (p. 339). So how could I, a Jewish woman, be implicated in the subordination of others? In those early moments, I had not stopped to interrogate my own white privilege and my own contributions to systematic oppression. Racing to innocence, however unintentionally, softened my re-entry into the classroom and, thus, provided a temporary landing from which I could continue my reflexive journey.

HOW COULD I NOT …

As that academic year came to an end and the panoply of emotions became manageable, my reflexive journey continued with concerns of how I could use these experiences and reflections to decolonize knowledge production in academic spaces. But first, I interrogated my "academic" privilege and my complicity, through claims of ignorance, in reproducing epistemic violence.

I was hired many years ago specifically for the research expertise acquired in my doctoral education. During my doctoral studies, I was deeply immersed in the positivist/empiricist epistemology. Post-theories that challenge the notion of research as a search for "the truth" were not on the academic radar at the time, with qualitative methodologies being the hotbed of debate. As an epistemology, positivism presents a theory of knowledge and knowledge production that answers questions about what counts as knowledge and who the "knower" is (Strega, 2005, p. 201). Positivism lays claim to knowledge as universal truths that are discovered through the rigorous and systematic application of the scientific method by an unbiased expert. When applied to social sciences, Neuman (2006) defines positivism as "an organized method for combining deductive logic with precise empirical observations of individual behaviour in order to discover and confirm a set of probabilistic causal laws that can be used to predict general patterns of human activity" (p. 82). The knowledge that arises from the scientific method is judged against the positivist trilogy of researcher objectivity, reliability, and validity. The ultimate purpose of positivist, and of the more recent post-positivist research, is an explanation that leads to prediction and control of human behaviour. Social phenomena are thus identified, measured, categorized, and subjected to universalized theories of human behaviour by a supposedly objective, detached, and dehistoricized researcher (Strega, 2005).

Knowledge arrived at in this manner is considered superior to all other knowledge. Positivism is positioned as an all-encompassing, totalized scientific research paradigm that excludes, denies, and is intolerant of all other ways of knowing, and thus acts as a "fascist structure" (Holmes, Murray, Perron, & Rail, 2006, p. 181). Holmes and colleagues (2006) write about the dominance of the evidence-based discourse within the health sciences, a discourse representing positivism. They argue that this discourse operates as a fascist regime in its "desire to order, hierarchize, control, repress, direct and impose limits" and achieve "the total subjection of humanity to the political imperatives of systems whose concerns are of their own production" (p. 184).

Upon entering the academy after completing my doctorate, it wasn't difficult to embrace the academic imperative that inscribes the dominance of positivist knowledge creation. As a totalizing regime, positivist-informed research is rewarded by funding bodies, academic journals, and by our own institution's awards practices. I justified these rewards by maintaining that I was using the tools of positivism to promote a social justice agenda. I also took comfort in using mixed-method and participatory designs. I managed to carve out a space for the voices of participants within the confines of positivism. Projects that include mixed methodologies may escape some of the critiques of positivism and contribute to social justice goals (see Pyne, Bauer, Hammond, & Travers, this volume), particularly when researchers infuse critical reflexivity and position their subjectivities within the process. These are themes that I take up later in this chapter.

The undergraduate research courses that I taught reflected a positivist orientation. At the time, however, I did not recognize the full extent of this positivist frame. In hindsight, the research texts that I used positioned positivism as *one* of many paradigms, with the two other primary paradigms at the time being interpretive and critical. I could thus settle into either of these other spaces and feel that I had moved away from positivist knowledge claims. This was a shift that I relished as I was questioning and feeling a discomfort with positivism's preoccupation with measurement and with the psychometric constructs used to represent human conditions, emotions, and behaviours. It was not until much later that I began to engage with critical constructionist scholarship. I recognized that interpretive and critical paradigms represented in traditional social work research texts were framed within a modernist epistemology and so perpetuated the dominance of positivist knowledge claims.

Given the hegemony of positivist epistemology, Strega (2005) argues that it is "successfully positioned as the most legitimate way to view the world" (p. 201) and thus becomes the standard against which other ways of knowing are held up. So while I may have tinkered with its methods, I had fully subscribed to its knowledge claims and to its "truths." I had dehistoricized research by ignoring its historical context. I had also removed my "self" from this content. I did not recognize the "constitutive powers of our histories" (herising, 2005), which resulted in my reproducing this colonial history. Many years later, it should not have come as such a surprise that my positivist epistemological roots were revealed in my categorization of the sharing circle in the focus group category.

My complicity in perpetuating colonialism thus stems from, but is not justified by, a "we do not even know that we do not know" type of ignorance (Tuana, 2006, p. 6). Tuana argues that this type of ignorance occurs when various topics are "obscured" by "interests, beliefs and theories" to which we ascribe (p. 6). Being entrenched in positivism, and claiming its rewards, I obscured and did not make room for Indigenous ways of knowing. This ignorance inevitably resulted in reproducing epistemic violence.

The Positivist Gaze

Gazing at the research subject through a positivist scientific lens has constituted one of the "worst excesses of colonialism" (Smith, 2012, p. 1). Smith describes the totalizing effect of Western positivism in that

> it is research which brings to bear, on any study of indigenous peoples, a cultural orientation, a set of values, a different conceptualization of such things as time, space and subjectivity, different and competing theories of knowledge, highly specialized forms of language, and structures of power. (p. 44)

Western knowledge provides the "procedures by which indigenous peoples and their societies were coded into the Western system of knowledge," denying and marginalizing all other ways of knowing (Smith, 2012, p. 45). As Trinder (1996) reminds us, "research perspectives are not ahistorical and methodologies are not innocent sets of techniques" (p. 234). Instead, they are "instruments for legitimating various colonial practices" that are intended to entrench Western ways of knowing and being (Smith, 2012, p. 60). Western knowledge is thus positioned as ahistorical and universally applicable knowledge (Connell, 2007; see also El-Lahib, this volume).

Researchers steeped within Western ways of knowing construct the "other" through acts of representation and domination (Madison, 2005, p. 7). Quijano (2000) talks of a Eurocentric "mirror that distorts what it reflects," producing "partial and distorted" images of the "other" (p. 556). These acts of representation have significant consequences, in that "how people are represented is how they are treated" (Madison, 2005, p. 4). Hence, Baskin (2005b) explicitly maintains that "an agenda for Aboriginal research must focus on the goals and processes of decolonization and self-determination. A research project that does not contribute in some way to these objectives is not worth doing" (para. 6). Smith (2012) defines decolonization as "the centring of our [Indigenous] concerns and world views and then coming to know and understand theory and research from our own perspectives and for our own purposes" (p. 41). Thus, research becomes a site of struggle, an escape from the Western gaze, and a path to reclaim Indigenous ways of knowing.

DECOLONIZING KNOWLEDGE PRODUCTION

Given the impact of research on marginal knowledges, the graduate research course becomes a very significant space in which to begin the process of decolonizing knowledge production. But how do I enter into this space? How do I engage and attend to the processes of colonization that exclude, marginalize, and appropriate Aboriginal knowledges, ideas, and practices (Hart, 2009)?

Baskin (2005a), Lavallée (2009), and Kovach (2005) speak of the challenges in bringing an Indigenous framework to the academy. Baskin (2005a) asks why Aboriginal research methodology must be accountable to the standards of the dominant society and not accepted as a legitimate form of research. Recognizing the constitutive nature of language, Kovach (2005) speaks of the difficulties in using Western concepts to describe Indigenous frameworks. Lavallée (2009) writes of her doctoral journey in which she used an Indigenous research framework. Lavallée shares her frustration of needing to justify Indigenous methods by comparing them to Western methods. Hill Collins (as cited in Baskin, 2005a), summarizes these challenges by stating that:

> Oppressed groups are frequently placed in the situation of being listened to only if we frame our ideas in the language that is familiar to and comfortable for a dominant group. This requirement often changes the meaning of our ideas and works to elevate the ideas of dominant groups. (para. 3)

How might we begin the process of decolonization when we are stuck using Western epistemologies and research methods? It seems as though efforts to unsettle Western epistemology seem to re-inscribe its dominance yet again. It becomes critically necessary to interrogate and unsettle the "underlying and obscure operations of power and control" (Madison, 2005, p. 5) that are rooted in processes of knowledge production. As cautioned by Holmes and colleagues (2006), it requires deconstruction work that "demonstrates how concepts or ideas are contingent upon historical, linguistic, social and political discourses" (p. 182). These are some of the challenges I struggled with during that summer. I began to realize that teaching students about the different research methods and frameworks does not constitute the critical pedagogy required to address the epistemological questions that framed the course. So while I was on the right track in framing the course, I had not created a space that allowed for a critical engagement with these questions. I came to understand that the course needed to be built around concepts that would help students think about research critically, historically, and reflexively. I selected three concepts that I felt would assist us in repositioning and decolonizing research: (1) subjectivity, (2) representation, and (3) positionality. These critical and interrelated concepts would help us interrogate not only what we know but also how we come to know it. These concepts take up uncomfortable issues and challenge us to engage in reflective and implicating questions.

I take up the concept of subjectivity with questions such as: How am I historically, culturally, politically, and institutionally positioned in relation to those whom I am studying? How are my "shifting subjectivities" implicated, historically and currently, in various forms of subjugation (herising, 2005, p. 147)?

I approach the concept of research as representation by asking questions: If research constitutes an act of representation, then who do I have the right to represent? Can I represent any truth other than my own (Absolon & Willett, 2005)? How do my acts of representation constitute acts of domination (Madison, 2005)?

I engage with the concept of researcher positionality by asking: What right do I have to enter communities of which I am not a member? What are the consequences of using my "Western eyes" to represent the "other" (Mohanty, 2002)? How am I positioned in perpetuating or breaking hegemonic power and knowledge (Bhattacharya, 2008)? Am I "creating space or taking away space" through the research process (Kovach, 2005, p. 26)?

Consequently, this reflective questioning more directly speaks to, and interrogates, the epistemological questions that inform the course. I felt as though I was now getting closer to connecting the intentions of the course with its pedagogy.

To support the integration of these concepts and reflective questions, I developed a critical essay assignment, which I called "Repositioning Social Work Research." In this assignment students were asked to discuss how these concepts can be used in social work research to challenge and reposition power relations, unsettle dominant representations, and contribute to anti-oppression practice. I eliminated the group "methods" presentations, replacing them with group presentations in which students were asked to develop a research proposal that addressed these challenges. In the final assignment, I asked students to identify an aspect of their research proposals that was "troubling" and how they will engage with this issue when undertaking their own future research projects.

Going back into the research class the next academic year was very difficult. Though I felt that I had done some significant self-work that summer, I was filled with self-doubt. How might the roots of my positivism, not reached by this beginning critical reflection, be revealed yet again? Would I be perceived as authentic in attempting to reposition social work research?

Reconceptualizing the course, however, did provide a set of reflective questions that directly frame decolonization as a process and as a journey: one that is bumpy and winding, but also directional. Anticipating a bumpy ride helps to create a space of learning, of risk-taking, and of developing a critical self-awareness. As students began to engage with these concepts, an emotional and intellectual passion became increasingly apparent. The intensity of the students' engagement with this material was one that I had not experienced in a research course before. My sense is that by collectively and individually struggling with these ideas and implicating ourselves in these contexts, we were able to begin the process of decolonizing our understanding of research and repositioning ourselves in relation to its processes and outcomes. We were beginning to "undo" research as we had come to understand it and starting our journeys of positioning research as an act of resistance and as a site of recovery (Brown & Strega, 2005). We were in the processes of becoming anti-oppressive researchers (Potts & Brown, 2005).

CONCLUSION

My reflexive journey began as a result of my relationship with Indigenous research methodologies, and so I will end this critical autoethnography by sharing some thoughts on the journey that I continue. I hold onto the challenge put forth by Simpson (as cited in Hart, 2009), stating that:

> Academics and new learners who are to be true allies to Indigenous Peoples in the protection of our knowledge must be willing to step outside of their privileged position and challenge research that conforms to the guidelines outlined by the

colonial power structure and root their work in the politics of decolonization and anti-colonialism. (p. 31)

Working within this politics requires that anti-oppression researchers "have a critical understanding of colonialism and an understanding of Western scientific research as a mechanism of colonization" (Absolon & Willett, 2005, p. 120).

I have come to respect and understand the significance of Indigenous epistemologies and research methodologies in the struggle toward self-determination and recovery. In classroom spaces, I centre this purpose, as it is no longer fully obscured by an unchallenged positivism. In these spaces, I do not try to represent Indigenous epistemologies and research methodologies. I can only represent my relationship with these methodologies. I draw on Indigenous scholarship so that my students and I can learn "first" voice perspectives on how we can contribute to the processes of decolonizing research. I take up these issues by "speaking about," but not "on behalf of First Peoples" (Hulan & Warley, 1999, p. 67). I seek guidance from Indigenous practitioners as to how we must enter and work with Aboriginal communities. Akiwenzie-Damm describes how we might join the circle and states that we have a "responsibility to join the circle humbly, to listen actively, accept responsibility, to become more informed, to recognize our complacency, to face our pasts, to remember, to confront the vestiges of imperialist thought" (as quoted in Hulan & Warley, 1999, p. 69). How we enter the circle thus becomes a powerful metaphor of the stance we must take as researchers, educators, and practitioners when working with Indigenous Peoples and communities.

As universities continue to reflect colonial practices, bringing Indigenous epistemologies to the centre is an ongoing challenge, one to which all allies need to fully subscribe. Dei (2000) reminds us that "to integrate Indigenous knowledges into Western academies is to recognize that different knowledges can co-exist, that different knowledges can complement each other and also that knowledges can be in conflict at the same time" (p. 120). This speaks to a critical pedagogy that "privileges multiple subject positions, questions its own authority, and doubts those narratives that privilege one set of historical processes and sequences over another" (McLaren, as quoted in Denzin, 2003b, p. 268).

In conclusion, I began this reflexive journey based on an act of "epistemic violence" that I committed against Indigenous knowledges. My early responses were emotional and spiritual, as I sought comfort and reassurance through claims of innocence. I then moved toward a narrative of ignorance as I placed blame on my positivist foundations. I was finally able to begin moving away from the immobilizing spaces of innocence and ignorance and toward a politics of anti-colonialism.

As I continue along my reflective journey and the deep personal excavating that this entails, I embrace critical pedagogy, however tenuous, that we can hold in the midst of our colonial institutions. I search for ways in which I can bring bell hooks's (1994) vision of education as the practice of freedom to my classrooms, and where my classrooms can contribute to those spaces for what Daniel Justice (2004) calls "significant cultural recovery work" (p. 102). Bringing Indigenous knowledges in from the margins of the academy and from the thresholds of our classrooms will move us closer to making this vision a reality.

References

Absolon, K., & Willett, C. (2005). Putting ourselves forward: Location in Aboriginal research. In L. Brown & S. Strega (Eds.), *Research as resistance: Critical, indigenous, & anti-oppressive approaches* (pp. 97–126). Toronto, ON: Canadian Scholars' Press.

Activating Change Together for Community Food Security (ACT for CFS). (2014). *Knowledge mobilization in participatory action research: A synthesis of the literature.* Halifax, NS: Food ARC, Mount Saint Vincent University.

Adams, H. (1999). *Tortured people: The politics of colonization.* Penticton, BC: Theytus Books.

Adams, P., & Chandler, S. M. (2004). Responsive regulation in child welfare: Systemic challenges to mainstreaming the Family Group Conference. *Journal of Sociology and Social Welfare, 31*(1), 93–116.

Ahmed, S. (2012). *On being included: Racism and diversity in institutional life.* Durham, NC: Duke University Press.

Alcoff, L. (1991/1992). The problem of speaking for others. *Cultural Critique, 20*, 5–32.

Allen, R. L. (2001). The globalization of white supremacy: Toward a critical discourse on the racialization of the world. *Educational Theory, 51*(4), 467–485.

Allison, C. B. (2000). Okie narratives: Agency and whiteness. In J. L. Kincheloe, S. R. Steinberg, N. M. Rodriguez, & R. E. Chennault (Eds.), *White reign: Deploying whiteness in America* (pp. 229–240). Durham, NC: Duke University Press.

American Psychiatric Association. (2012). *Sexual and gender identity disorders.* Retrieved from http://www.dsm5.org/meetus/pages/sexualandgenderidentitydisorders.aspx

Ansara, Y. G., & Hegarty, P. (2011). Cisgenderism in psychology: Pathologizing and misgendering children from 1999 to 2008. *Psychology & Sexuality, 3*(2), 137–160.

Anzaldúa, G. (1987). *Borderlands/La Frontera: The new mestizo.* San Francisco, CA: Aunt Lute Books.

Arai, S., & Kivel, D. B. (2009). Critical race theory and social justice perspectives on whiteness, difference(s) and (anti)racism: A fourth wave of race research in leisure studies. *Journal of Leisure Research, 41*(4), 459–472.

Aronson, J., & Sammon, S. (2000). Practice amid social service cuts and restructuring: Working with the contradictions of small victories. *Canadian Social Work Review, 17*(2), 167–187.

Aronson, J., & Smith, K. (2010). Managing restructured social services: Expanding the social? *British Journal of Social Work, 40*(20), 530–547.

Bailey, A. (1999). Despising an identity they taught me to claim: Exploring a dilemma of white privilege awareness. In C. J. Cuomo & K. Q. Hall (Eds.), *Whiteness: Feminist philosophical narratives* (pp. 85–104). Lanham, MD: Rowman & Littlefield.

Baines, D. (2000). Everyday practices of race, class and gender: Struggles, skills and radical social work. *Journal of Progressive Human Services, 11*(2), 5–27.

Baines, D. (2002). Storylines in racialized times: Racism and anti-racism in Toronto's social services. *British Journal of Social Work, 32*, 185–199.

Baines, D. (2004a). Seven kinds of work—only one paid: Raced, gendered and restructured work in social services. *Atlantis, 28*(2), 19–28.

Baines, D. (2004b). Pro-market, non-market: The duel nature of organizational change in social services delivery. *Critical Social Policy, 24*(1), 5–29.

Baines, D. (2007). Anti-oppressive social work practice: Fighting for space, fighting for change. In D. Baines (Ed.), *Doing anti-oppressive practice: Building transformative, politicized social work* (pp. 13–42). Halifax, NS: Fernwood Publishing.

Baines, D. (2011a). An overview of anti-oppressive practice: Roots, theory, tensions. In D. Baines (Ed.), *Doing anti-oppressive practice: Building transformative, politicized social work* (2nd ed., pp. 1–24). Halifax, NS: Fernwood Publishing.

Baines, D. (2011b). Building the practice-activism divide in mainstream social work. In D. Baines (Ed.), *Doing anti-oppressive practice: Building transformative, politicized social work* (2nd ed., pp. 79–94). Halifax, NS: Fernwood Publishing.

Baines, S., & Edwards, J. (2015). Considering the ways in which anti-oppressive practice principles can inform health research. *The Arts in Psychotherapy, 42*, 28–34.

Bakker, A., van Kesteren, P., Gooren, L., & Bezemer, P. (1993). The prevalence of transsexualism in The Netherlands. *Acta Psychiatrica Scandinavica, 87*(4), 237–238.

Baldwin, A. (2012). Whiteness and futurity: Towards a research agenda. *Progress in Human Geography, 36*, 508–517.

Ball, M. S., & Smith, G. H. (1992). *Analyzing visual data.* Newbury Park, CA: Sage.

Banks, M. (2001). *Visual methods in social research.* Thousand Oaks, CA: Sage.

Bansel, P., Davies, B., Gannon, S., & Linnell, S. (2008). Technologies of audit at work on the writing subject: A discursive analysis. *Studies in Higher Education, 33*(6), 673–683.

Barker, C., & Murray, S. (2010). Disabling postcolonialism: Global disability cultures and democratic criticism. *Journal of Literary & Cultural Disability Studies, 4*(3), 219–236.

Barnes, C., & Mercer, G. (1997). *Doing disability research.* Leeds: The Disability Press.

Barnes, C., & Mercer, G. (2003). *Disability.* Cambridge: Polity Press.

Barnes, C., & Mercer, G. (2006). Researching user-led organizations. In C. Barnes & G. Mercer (Eds.), *Independent futures: Creating user-led disability services in a disabling society* (pp. 51–68). Bristol, UK: Polity Press.

Barnoff, L. (2001). Moving beyond words: Integrating anti-oppression practice into feminist social services. *Canadian Social Work Review, 18*, 67–86.

Barnoff, L. (2002). New directions for anti-oppression practice in feminist social service agencies. (Unpublished doctoral dissertation). University of Toronto, Canada.

Barnoff, L., George, P., & Coleman, B. (2006). Operating in "survival mode": Challenges to implementing anti-oppressive practice in feminist social service agencies in Toronto. *Canadian Social Work Review, 23*(1), 41–58.

Barnoff, L., & Moffatt, K. (2007). Contradictory tensions in anti-oppression practice in feminist social services. *Affilia: Journal of Women and Social Work, 22*(1), 56–70.

Barnoff, L., Parada, H., & Grassau, P. (2004). *Transforming social work: Creating space for anti-oppression and social justice practices: Conference report.* Toronto, ON: School of Social Work, Ryerson University.

Bartels, L. (2004). Some unfulfilled promises of quantitative imperialism. In H. E. Brady & D. Collier (Eds.), *Rethinking social inquiry: Diverse tools, shared standards* (pp. 83–88). Lanham, MD: Rowman & Littlefield.

Barthes, R. (1982). Myth today. In S. Sontag (Ed.), *A Barthes reader* (pp. 93–149). New York, NY: Hill and Wang.

Baskin, C. (2005a). Storytelling circles: Reflections of Aboriginal protocols in research. *Canadian Social Work Review, 22*(2), 171–187.

Baskin, C. (2005b). Gathering stories: Aboriginal research methodologies. *Canadian Social Work Review, 22*(2), 171–189.

Baskin, C. (2006). Aboriginal world views as challenges and possibilities in social work education. *Critical Social Work, 7*(2). Retrieved from http://www1.uwindsor.ca/criticalsocialwork/

Baskin, C. (2011). *Strong helpers' teachings: The value of Indigenous knowledges in the helping professions.* Toronto, ON: Canadian Scholars' Press.

Bauer, G. (2012, September 23). *Developing knowledge on trans health in Canada.* Keynote delivered to Canadian Professional Association for Transgender Health Conference. Winnipeg, MB.

Bauer, G., Hammond, R., Travers, R., Kaay, M., Hohenadel, K., & Boyce, M. (2009). "I don't think this is theoretical; this is our lives": How erasure impacts health care for transgender people. *Journal of the Association of Nurses in AIDS Care, 20*(5), 348–361.

Bauer, G., Pyne, J., Francino, M., & Hammond, R. (2013). Suicidality among trans people in Ontario: Implications for social work and social justice. *Service Social, 59*(1), 35–62.

Bauer, G., Scheim, A., Deutsch, M., & Massarella, C. (2014). Reported emergency department avoidance, utilization and experiences of transgender persons in Ontario, Canada: Results from a respondent-driven sampling survey. *Annals of Emergency Medicine, 63*(6), 713–720.

128 | References

Bauer, G. R., Travers, R., Scanlon, K., & Coleman T. A. (2012). High heterogeneity of HIV-related sexual risk among transgender people in Ontario, Canada: A province-wide respondent-driven sampling survey. *BMC Public Health, 12*(1), 292.

Baumbusch, J. L., Kirkham, S. R., Khan, K. B., McDonald, H., Semeniuk, P., Tan, E., & Anderson, J. M. (2008). Pursuing common agendas: A collaborative model for knowledge translation between research and practice in clinical settings. *Research in Nursing & Health, 31*(2), 130–140.

Beck, N. (2006). Is causal-process observation an oxymoron? *Political Analysis, 14*(3), 347–352.

Bennet, A., & Bennet, D. (2008). *Knowledge mobilization in the social sciences and humanities: Moving from research to action.* Frost, WV: MQI Press.

Berg, L. (2012). Geographies of identity I: Geography–(neo)liberalism–white supremacy. *Progress in Human Geography, 36*(4), 508–517.

Bery, S. (2014). Multiculturalism, teaching slavery, and white supremacy. *Equity and Excellence in Education, 47*, 334–352.

Bhabha, H. K. (2010). *The location of culture* (7th ed.). New York, NY: Routledge.

Bhattacharya, H. (2008). New critical collaborative ethnography. In S. N. Hess-Biber & P. Leavy (Eds.), *Handbook of emergent methods* (pp. 303–324). New York, NY: Guilford Press.

Bishop, A. (2005). *Beyond token change: Breaking the cycle of oppression in institutions.* Halifax, NS: Fernwood Publishing.

Bishop, C. (2006a). Introduction: Viewers as producers. In C. Bishop (Ed.), *Participation* (pp. 10–17). Cambridge, MA: MIT Press.

Bishop, C. (2006b). The social turn: Collaboration and its discontents. *Artforum, 44*(6), 178–183.

Blanchard, K. (2010). Mastering the art of change: Ken Blanchard offers some strategies for successfully leading change. *Training Journal*, 44–47.

Blanchard, R. (1985). Typology of male-to-female transsexualism. *Archives of Sexual Behavior, 14*, 247–261.

Boehm, A. (2004). Integrating media and community practice: A case of television report production. *Social Work Education, 23*(4), 417–434.

Boston, T. (2009). *Understanding Thorncliffe Park: Needs assessment report.* Retrieved from http://www.cscleaders.org/media/2667/Thorncliffe%20NO%20 -%20needs-assessment-final-report-dec-15-2009.pdf

Boylorn, R. (2011). Gray or for coloured girls who are tired of chasing rainbows: Race and reflexivity. *Cultural Studies <=> Critical Methodologies, 11*(2), 178–186.

Bradley, S., Blanchard, R., Coates, S., Levine, S., Meyer-Bahlburg., H, Pauly., I., & Zucker, K. (1991). Interim report of the DSM-IV Subcommittee on Gender Identity Disorders. *Archives of Sexual Behaviour, 20*(4), 333–343.

Briggs, G., Briggs, A., Whitmore, E., Maki, A., Ackerley, C., & Maisonneuve, A. (2015). *Questing your way to a knowledge mobilization strategy.* Ottawa, ON: Social Sciences and Humanities Research Council.

Broner, N., Franczak, M., Dye, C., & McAllister, W. (2001). Knowledge transfer, policymaking and community empowerment: A consensus model approach for providing public mental health and substance abuse services. *Psychiatric Quarterly, 72*(1), 79–102.

Brown, C. (2009). WWW.HATE.COM: White supremacist discourse on the internet and the construction of whiteness ideology. *The Howard Journal of Communications, 20*, 189–208.

Brown, L., & Strega, S. (2005). Introduction: Transgressive possibilities. In L. Brown & S. Strega (Eds.), *Research as resistance: Critical, Indigenous and anti-oppressive approaches* (pp. 1–17). Toronto, ON: Canadian Scholars' Press.

Bryman, A. (2008). *Social research methods* (3rd ed.). New York, NY: Oxford University Press.

Buchignani, N. (2010). South Asian Canadians. In J. Marsh (Ed.), *The Canadian encyclopedia.* Retrieved from http://www.thecanadianencyclopedia.ca/en/article/south-asians/

Burke, P. (1996). *Gender shock: Exploding the myths of male and female.* New York, NY: Anchor Books.

Burns, P. M. (2004). Six postcards from Arabia: A visual discourse of colonial travels in the Orient. *Tourist Studies, 4*, 255–275.

Bush, B. (2006). *Imperialism and postcolonialism. History: Concepts, theories and practice.* Toronto, ON: Pearson Education.

Bussières, D., Dumais, L., Fontan, J-M., Lapierre, A., Shields, G., Sutton, L., & Vaillancourt, S. (2008). *Guide for knowledge mobilization in the context of research partnerships.* Montreal, QC: Canadian Social Economy Research Partners.

Butler, J. (1990). *Gender trouble: Feminism and the subversion of identity.* New York, NY: Routledge.

Butler, J. (1997). *The psychic life of power. Theories in subjection.* Stanford, CA: Stanford University Press.

Calafell, B. M. (2013). (I)dentities: Considering accountability, reflexivity and intersectionality in the I and the We. *Liminalities: A Journal of Performance Studies, 9*(2), 6–13.

Cameron, C. (2007). Whose problem? Disability narratives and available identities. *Community Development Journal, 42*(4), 501–511.

Campbell, C. (2003). Anti-oppressive theory and practice as the organizing theme for social work education: The case in favour. *Canadian Social Work Review, 20*, 121–125.

Canadian Institutes of Health Research (CIHR). (2004). *Innovation in action. Knowledge Translation Strategy 2004–2009*. Retrieved from http://www.cihr-irsc.gc.ca/e/26574.html

Chambon, A. (2008). Social work and the arts: Critical imagination. In J. G. Knowles & A. L. Cole (Eds.), *Handbook of the arts in qualitative research* (pp. 591–602). London: Sage.

Chataika, T. (2012). Disability, development and postcolonialism. In D. Goodley, B. Hughes & L. Davis (Eds.), *Disability and social theory: New developments and directions* (pp. 252–269). New York, NY: Palgrave Macmillan.

Chilisa, B. (2012). *Indigenous research methodologies*. Los Angeles, CA: Sage.

City of Toronto. (2006a). *Flemingdon Park neighbourhood profiles*. Retrieved from http://www.toronto.ca/demographics/cns_profiles/cns44.htm

City of Toronto. (2006b). *Thorncliffe Park neighbourhood profiles*. Retrieved from http://www.toronto.ca/demographics/cns_profiles/cns55.htm

Clover, D., & Craig, C. (2009). Street-life's creative turn: An exploration of arts-based adult education and knowledge mobilization with homeless/street-involved women in Victoria. *Canadian Journal for the Study of Adult Education, 22*(1), 21–35.

Clover, D., & Stalker, J. (2005). Social justice, arts and adult education. *Convergence, 38*(4), 3–7.

Comor, E. (2008). *Consumption and the globalization project: International hegemony and the annihilation of time*. New York, NY: Palgrave Macmillan.

Connell, R. (2007). *Southern theory: The global dynamics of knowledge in social science*. Cambridge: Polity Press.

Connell, R. (2011). Southern bodies and disability: Re-thinking concepts. *Third World Quarterly, 32*(8), 1369–1381.

Crenshaw, K. (1991). Mapping the margins: Intersectionality, identity, politics and violence against women of color. *Stanford Law Review, 43*, 1241–1299.

Creswell, J. W. (2013). *Qualitative inquiry and research design: Choosing among five approaches* (3rd ed.). Thousand Oaks, CA: Sage.

Crist, J. D., & Tanner, C. A. (2003). Interpretation/analysis methods in hermeneutic interpretive phenomenology. *Nursing Research, 52*(3), 202–205.

Currah, P., & Stryker, S. (2015). Introduction. *Transgender Studies Quarterly, 2*(1), 1–12.

Daly, M. (1978). *Gyn/ecology: The metaethics of radical feminism*. Boston, MA: Beacon Press.

Davies, B. (2000). *A body of writing. 1990–1999*. Walnut Creek, CA: AltaMira Press.

Davies, B. (2005). The (im)possibility of intellectual work in neoliberal regimes. *Discourse: Studies in the Cultural Politics of Education, 26*(1), 1–14.

Davison, C. M., & National Collaborating Centre for Determinants of Health (NCCDH). (2013). *Critical examination of knowledge to action models and implication for promoting health equity.* Retrieved from http://nccdh.ca/resources/entry/critical-examination-of-knowledge-to-action-models#sthash.JM60CwxL.dpuf

Dei, G. S. (1999). The denial of difference: Reframing anti-racist praxis. *Race, Ethnicity and Education, 2*(1), 17–37.

Dei, G. S. (2000). Rethinking the role of Indigenous knowledges in the academy. *International Journal of Inclusive Education, 4*(3), 111–132.

Dei, G. S., & Johal, G. S. (Eds). (2005). *Anti-racist research methodologies.* New York, NY: Peter Lang.

Denny, D. (1992). The politics of diagnosis and a diagnosis of politics. The university-affiliated gender clinics and how they failed to meet the needs of transsexual people. *Chrysalis Quarterly, 1*(3), 9–20.

Denny, D. (1994). *Gender dysphoria: A guide to research.* New York, NY: Garland Press.

Denzin, N.K. (2003a). *Performance ethnography: Critical pedagogy and the politics of culture.* Thousand Oaks, CA: Sage.

Denzin, N. K. (2003b). Performing [auto]ethnography politically. *Review of Education, Pedagogy, and Cultural Studies, 25*(3), 257–278.

Denzin, N. K., & Lincoln, Y. S. (2005). The discipline and practice of qualitative research. In N. K. Denzin & Y. S. Lincoln (Eds.), *The Sage handbook of qualitative research* (3rd ed., pp. 1–32). Thousand Oaks, CA: Sage.

Dingo, R. (2007). Making the "unfit, fit": The rhetoric of mainstreaming in the World Bank's commitment to gender equality and disability rights. *Wagadu, 4*, 93–107.

Dominelli, L. (1999). Neo-liberalism, social exclusion and welfare clients in a global economy. *International Journal of Social Welfare, 8*, 14–22.

Dominelli, L. (2002a). Anti-oppressive practice in context. In R. Adams, L. Dominelli, & M. Payne (Eds.), *Social work: Themes, issues, and critical debates* (2nd ed., pp. 3–19). Basingstoke, UK: Palgrave Macmillan.

Dominelli, L. (2002b). *Anti-oppressive social work theory and practice.* Basingstoke, UK: Palgrave Macmillan.

Dominelli, L. (2009). Social work research: Contested knowledge for practice. In R. Adams, L. Dominelli, & M. Payne (Eds.), *Practising social work in a complex world* (pp. 240–255). Basingstoke, UK: Palgrave.

Dossa, P. (2006). Disability, marginality and the nation-state—negotiating social markers of difference: Fahimeh's story. *Disability and Society, 21*(4), 345–358.

Dossa, P. (2009). *Racialized bodies, disabling worlds: Storied lives of immigrant Muslim women.* Toronto, ON: University of Toronto Press.

Dowling, M. (2007). From Husserl to van Manen: A review of different phenomenological approaches. *International Journal of Nursing Studies, 44*(1), 131–142.

Drew, N. (2004). Creating a synthesis of intentionality: The role of the bracketing facilitator. *Advances in Nursing Science, 27*(3), 215–223.

Dubois, W. E. B. (1935). *Black reconstruction, 1860–1880.* New York, NY: Harcourt.

Dubois, W. E. B. (1969). *The souls of black folk.* New York, NY: Signet Classic.

Dubois, W. E. B. (1970). *The Philadelphia negro: A social study* (3rd ed.). New York, NY: Schocken Books.

Eastham, S., Negropontes, J., Walsh, C. A., Ciesielski, M., Harris, J., Jones, S., … & Aarestad, S. (2010). Out of the lower depths: The power of the arts for social justice transformation. *Reflections: Narratives of Professional Helping, 16*(3), 52–61.

Edwards, R. (1979). *Contested terrain.* London: Heinemann.

Eisner, E. (2008). Arts and knowledge. In J. G. Knowles & A. L. Cole (Eds.), *Handbook of arts in qualitative research* (pp. 3–12). Thousand Oaks, CA: Sage.

Ellis, C., & Bochner, A. P. (2000). Autoethnography, personal narrative, reflexivity: Research as subject. In N. K. Denzin & Y. S. Lincoln (Eds.), *The Sage handbook of qualitative research* (2nd ed., pp. 733–768). Thousand Oaks, CA: Sage.

Ellwood, P., Thorpe, R., & Coleman, C. (2013). A model for knowledge mobilization and implications for the education of social researchers. *Contemporary Social Science: Journal of the Academy of Social Sciences, 8*(3), 191–206.

Emmison, M., & Smith, P. (2000). *Researching the visual: Images, objects, contexts and interactions in social and cultural inquiry.* Thousand Oaks, CA: Sage.

Englander, M. (2012). The interview: Data collection in descriptive phenomenological human scientific research. *Journal of Phenomenological Psychology, 43*(1), 13–35.

Faulkner, S. (2013). Notes from a *Pretty Straight Girl*: Questioning identities in the field. *Liminalities: A Journal of Performance Studies, 9*(2), 39–48.

Fawcett, B., & Hearn, J. (2004). Researching others: Epistemology, experience, standpoints and participation. *International Journal of Social Research Methodology, 7*(3), 201–218.

Fellows, M. L., & Razack, S. (1998). The race to innocence: Confronting hierarchical relations among women. *Journal of Gender, Race & Justice, 1*, 335–352.

Felt, L., Rowe, P., & Curlew, K. (2004). *Teaching academic dogs and cats new tricks: "Re-tooling" senior academic researchers for collaborative community-based research.* Paper presented at the 10th Researching the Voluntary Sector Conference, Sheffield Hallam University, Sheffield.

Fine, M. (2006). Bearing witness: Methods for researching oppression and resistance—A textbook for critical research. *Social Justice Research, 19*(1), 83–108.

Finley, S. (2011). Critical arts-based inquiry: The pedagogy and performance of a radical ethical aesthetic. In N. K. Denzin & Y. S. Lincoln (Eds.), *The Sage handbook of qualitative research* (4th ed., pp. 435-450). Thousand Oaks, CA: Sage.

Fiske, J. (1998). Surveilling the city: Whiteness, the black man and democratic totalitarianism. *Theory, Culture & Society, 15*, 67–88.

Fitzgerald, T. (2004). Powerful voices and powerful stories: Reflections on the challenges and dynamics of intercultural research. *Journal of Intercultural Studies, 25*(3), 233–245.

Fitzpatrick, B. (2008). Atomic afterimages. *History of Photography, 32*(2), 176–187.

Flax, J. (1993). *Disputed subjects: Essays on psychoanalysis, politics and philosophy.* New York, NY: Routledge.

Flower, J., & Wirz, S. (2000). Rhetoric or reality? The participation of disabled people in NGO planning. *Health Policy and Planning, 15*(2), 177–185.

Floyd, M. F. (2007). Research on race and ethnicity in leisure: Anticipating the fourth wave. *Leisure/Loisir, 31*, 245–254.

Fook, J. (1993). *Radical casework: A theory of practice.* St. Leonards, NSW: Allen & Unwin.

Fook, J. (2012). *Social work: Critical theory and practice* (2nd ed.). London: Sage.

Fook, J., & Gardner, F. (2007). *Practising critical reflection: A handbook.* New York, NY: McGraw-Hill.

Foucault, M. (1986). Of other spaces. (T. Miskowiec, Trans.). *Diacritics, 16*(1), 22–27.

Foucault, M. (1991). Governmentality. In G. Burchell, C. Gordon, & P. Miller (Eds.), *The Foucault effect. Studies in governmentality. With two lectures by and an interview with Michel Foucault* (pp. 87–104). Chicago, IL: University of Chicago Press.

Foucault, M. (1994). Subjectivity and truth. In P. Rabinow (Ed.), *Michel Foucault. Ethics, subjectivity and truth. Essential works* (Vol. 1, pp. 87–92). New York, NY: New Press.

Foucault, M. (2000). The subject and power. In J. D. Faubion (Ed.), *Michel Foucault. Power. Essential works of Foucault 1954–1984* (Vol. 3, pp. 326–348). New York, NY: New Press.

Freire, P. (2000). *Pedagogy of the oppressed.* (M. Bergamn Ramos, Trans.). New York, NY: Continuum.

Friedman, M. (2013). *Mommyblogs and the changing face of motherhood.* Toronto, ON: University of Toronto Press.

Gabriel, J. (1998). *Whitewash: Racialized politics and the media.* London: Routledge.

Galabuzi, G. E. (2006). *Canada's economic apartheid: The social exclusion of racialized groups in the new century.* Toronto, ON: Canadian Scholars' Press.

Galabuzi, G. E., Das Gupta, T., James, C. E., Roger, C. A., & Andersen, C. (Eds.). (2007). *Race and racialization: Essential readings.* Toronto, ON: Canadian Scholars' Press.

Gapka, S., & Raj., R. (2003). *Trans health project.* Ontario Public Health Association. Retrieved from http://opha.on.ca/getmedia/166e2574-3eaf-4bfc-8c32-31a072d44233/2004-06_pp.pdf.aspx?ext=.pdf

Gearing, R. E. (2004). Bracketing in research: A typology. *Qualitative Health Research, 14*(10), 1429–1452.

Ghai, A. (2001). Disability in the Indian context: Post-colonial perspectives. In M. Corker & T. Shakespeare (Eds.), *Disability/postmodernity: Embodying disability theory* (pp. 89–100). New York, NY: Continuum.

Ghai, A. (2012). Engaging with disability with postcolonial theory. In D. Goodley, B. Hughes, & L. Davis (Eds.), *Disability and social theory: New developments and directions* (pp. 270–286). New York, NY: Palgrave Macmillan.

Gilroy, P. (1991). *"There ain't no black in the union jack": The cultural politics of race and nation.* London: University of Chicago Press.

Giorgi, A. (1994). A phenomenological perspective on certain qualitative research methods. *Journal of Phenomenological Psychology, 25*(2), 190–220.

Giorgi, A. (2008). Concerning a serious misunderstanding of the essence of the phenomenological methods in psychology. *Journal of Phenomenological Psychology, 39*(1), 33–58.

Giorgi, A. (2012). The descriptive phenomenological psychological method. *Journal of Phenomenological Psychology, 43*(1), 3–12.

Gonick, M., & Hladki, J. (2005). Who are the participants? Rethinking representational practices and writing with heterotopic possibility in qualitative inquiry. *International Journal of Qualitative Studies in Education, 18*(3), 285–304.

Goodley, D., Hughes, B., & Davis, L. (2012). Introducing disability and social theory. In D. Goodley, B. Hughes, & L. Davis (Eds.), *Disability and social theory: New developments and directions* (pp. 1–14). New York, NY: Palgrave Macmillan.

Goodley, D., & Lawthom, R. (2011). Disability, community and empire: Indigenous psychologies and the social psychoanalytic possibilities. *International Journal of Inclusive Education, 15*(1), 101–115.

Gordon, L. R. (1997). *Her majesty's other children: Sketches of racism from a neocolonial age.* Lanham, MD: Rowman & Littlefield.

Graham, H. (1983). Do her answers fit his questions? Women and the survey method. In E. Gamarnikow, D. Morgan, J. Purvis, & D. Taylorson (Eds.), *The public and the private* (pp. 132–147). London: Heinemann.

Gray, J. (2007). (Re)considering voice. *Qualitative Social Work, 6*(4), 411–430.

Grech, S. (2009). Disability, poverty and development: Critical reflections on the majority world debate. *Disability and Society, 24*(6), 771–784.

Grech, S. (2011). Disability and the majority world: Challenging dominant epistemologies. *Journal of Literary & Cultural Disability Studies, 5*(2), 217–219.

Grech S. (2012). Disability and the majority world: A neocolonial approach. In D. Goodley, B. Hughes, & L. Davis (Eds.), *Disability and social theory: New developments and directions* (pp. 52–69). New York, NY: Palgrave Macmillan.

Green, F., & Friedman, M. (2013). *Chasing rainbows: Exploring gender fluid parenting practices.* Toronto, ON: Demeter Press.

Green, R., & Money, J. (1969). *Transsexualism and sex reassignment.* Baltimore, MD: Johns Hopkins University Press.

Greene, S., & Chambers, L. (2011). The community-based research practicum as anti-oppressive social work education. In D. Baines (Ed.), *Doing anti-oppressive practice: Building transformative, politicized social work* (2nd ed., pp. 162–175). Halifax, NS: Fernwood Publishing.

Greer, G. (1999). *The whole woman*. London: Doubleday.

Groce, N. (2005). Immigrants, disability, and rehabilitation. In H. Stone (Ed.), *Culture and disability: Providing culturally competent services* (pp. 1–14). Thousand Oaks, CA: Sage.

Groenewald, T. (2004). A phenomenological research design illustrated. *International Journal of Qualitative Methods, 4*(1), 1–25.

Guberman, N., Lamoureux, J., Fournier, D., Beeman, J., & Gervais, L. (2003). Are the movement's organizations open to the movement's members? A study of democratic practices in women's groups in Quebec. *Resources for Feminist Research, 30*(1–2), 101–124.

Gutierrez, L., & Lewis, E. (1999). *Empowering women of color*. New York, NY: Columbia University Press.

Habermas, J. (1972). *Knowledge and human interests*. (J. J. Shapiro, Trans.). London: Heinemann.

Hacking, I. (2002). *Historical ontology*. Cambridge, MA: Harvard University Press.

Hafford-Letchfield, T., Leonard, K., & Couchman, W. (2012). "Arts and extremely dangerous": Critical commentary on the arts in social work education. *Social Work Education, 31*(6), 683–690.

Haig-Brown, C. (2009). Decolonizing diaspora: Whose traditional land are we on? *Cultural and Pedagogical Inquiry, 1*(1), 4–21.

Harper, D. (2004). Photography as social science data. In U. Flick, E. von Kardoff, & I. Steinke (Eds.), *A companion to qualitative research* (pp. 231–236). London: Sage.

Harrison, J., MacGibbon, L., & Morton, M. (2001). Regimes of trustworthiness in qualitative research: The rigors of reciprocity. *Qualitative Inquiry, 7*(3), 323–345.

Harrison-Quintana, J., Grant, J., & Rivera, I.G. (2015). Boxes of our own creation: A trans data collection wo/manifesto. *Transgender Studies Quarterly, 2*(1), 166–174.

Hart, J. G. (1997). The *summum bonum* and value-wholes: Aspects of a Husserlian axiology and theology. In J. G. Hart & L. Embree (Eds.), *Phenomenology of values and valuing* (pp. 193–230). Dordrecht, The Netherlands: Springer.

Hart, M. A. (2002). *Seeking Mino-Pimatisiwin: An Aboriginal approach to helping*. Halifax, NS: Fernwood Publishing.

Hart, M. A. (2009). Anti-colonial Indigenous social work: Reflections on an Aboriginal approach. In R. Sinclair, M. A. Hart, & G. Bruyere (Eds.), *Wicihitowin: Aboriginal social work in Canada* (pp. 25–41). Halifax, NS: Fernwood Publishing.

Hausman, B. (1995). *Changing sex: Transsexualism, technology and the idea of gender*. Durham, NC: Duke University Press.

Haynes, D., & White, B. (1999). Will the "real" social work please stand up? A call to stand for professional unity. *Social Work, 44*(4), 385–391.

Healy, K. (2000). *Social work practices: Contemporary perspectives on change.* London: Sage.

Heckathorn, D. (2002). Respondent-driven sampling II: Deriving valid population estimates from chain-referral samples of hidden populations. *Social Problems, 49,* 11–34.

Henry, F., & Tator, C. (2010). *The colour of democracy: Racism in Canadian society* (4th ed.). Toronto, ON: Harcourt.

herising, F. (2005). Interrupting positions: Critical thresholds and queer pro/positions. In L. Brown & S. Strega (Eds.), *Research as Resistance* (pp. 127–152). Toronto, ON: Canadian Scholars' Press.

Heron, G. (2004). Evidencing anti-racism in student assignments: Where has all the racism gone? *Qualitative Social Work, 3*(3), 277–295.

Heron, B. (2005). Self-reflection in critical social work practice: Subjectivity and the possibilities of resistance. *Reflective Practice, 6*(3), 341–351.

Heron, B. (2007). *Desire for development: Whiteness, gender, and the helping imperative.* Waterloo, ON: Wilfrid Laurier University Press.

Hick, S., & Pozzuto, R. (2005). Introduction: Towards "becoming" a critical social worker. In S. Hick, J. Fook, & R. Pozzuto (Eds.), *Social work. A critical turn* (pp. ix–xviii). Toronto, ON: Thompson Educational Publishing.

Hird, M. (2003). A typical gender identity conference? Some disturbing reports from the therapeutic front lines. *Feminism & Psychology, 13*(2), 181–199.

Hodder, I. (2000). The interpretation of documents and material culture. In N. K. Denzin & Y. S. Lincoln (Eds.), *Handbook of qualitative research* (2nd ed., pp. 703–715). Thousand Oaks, CA: Sage.

Hodson, R. (1995). Worker resistance: An underdeveloped concept in the sociology of work. *Economic and Industrial Democracy, 16,* 79–110.

Hoggett, P. (2001). Agency, rationality and social policy. *Journal of Social Policy, 30*(1), 37–56.

Hoggett, P., Beedell, P., Jimenez, L., Mayo, M., & Miller, C. (2006). Identity, life history and commitment to welfare. *Journal of Social Policy, 35*(4), 689–704.

Holden, C., & Beresford, P. (2002). Globalization and disability. In C. Barnes, M. Oliver, & L. Barton (Eds.), *Disability studies today* (pp. 190–209). Cambridge: Polity Press.

Holloway, I., & Todres, L. (2005). The status of method: Flexibility, consistency and coherence. In I. Holloway (Ed.), *Qualitative research in health care* (pp. 90–103). London: McGraw-Hill.

Hollway, W., & Jefferson, T. (2000). *Doing qualitative research differently: Free association, narrative and the interview method.* London: Sage.

Holmes, D., Murray, S., Perron, A., & Rail, G. (2006). Deconstructing the evidence-based discourse in health sciences: Truth, power and fascism. *International Journal of Evidence Based Health Care, 4,* 180–186.

Hoogvelt, A. (2001). *Globalization and the postcolonial world: The new political economy of development* (2nd ed.). Baltimore, MD: Johns Hopkins University Press.

hooks, b. (1994). *Teaching to transgress: Education as the practice of freedom*. New York, NY: Routledge.

Horwath, J., & Morrison, T. (2000). Identifying and implementing pathways for organizational change—Using the framework for the assessment of children in need and their families as a case example. *Child and Family Social Work, 5,* 245–254.

Huberdeau, R. (Dir. & Prod.). (2009). *Trans PULSE recruitment video*. Retrieved from https://www.youtube.com/watch?v=bqbVw4Vzpi4

Huff, D. D. (1998). Every picture tells a story. *Social Work, 43*(6), 576–583.

Hulan, R., & Warley, L. (1999). Cultural literacy, First Nations and the future of Canadian literacy studies. *Journal of Canadian Studies, 34*(3), 59–86.

Humphrey, C. (2007). Insider-outsider: Activating the hyphen. *Action Research, 5*(1), 11–26.

Huss, E. (2009). A case study of Bedouin women's art in social work: A model of social arts intervention with "traditional" women negotiating Western cultures. *Social Work Education, 28*(6), 598–616.

Huss, E. (2012). Utilizing an image to evaluate stress and coping for social workers. *Social Work Education, 31*(6), 691–702.

Huygens, I. (2001). Feminist attempts at power sharing in Aotearoa: Embarrassing herstory or significant learning towards treaty-based structures? *Feminism & Psychology, 11*, 393–400.

Hyde, C. (2004). Multicultural development in human services agencies: Challenges and solutions. *Social Work, 49*, 7–16.

Jacobson, N., Ochocka, J., Wise, J., Janzen, R., & Taking Culture Seriously Partners. (2007). Inspiring knowledge mobilization through a communications policy: The case of a community university research alliance. *Progress in Community Health Partnerships, Research, Education, and Action, 1*(1), 99–104.

Jermier, J. M., Knights, D., & Nord, W. R. (Eds.). (1994). *Resistance and power in organizations*. New York, NY: Routledge.

Jones, R. G. (2010). Putting privilege into practice through "Intersectional Reflexivity": Rumination, interventions, and possibilities. *Reflections: Narratives of Professional Helping, 16*, 122–125.

Justice, D. H. (2004). Seeing (and reading) Red: Indian outlaws in the Ivory Tower. In D. A. Mihesuah & A. C. Wilson (Eds.), *Indigenizing the academy: Transforming scholarship and empowering communities* (pp. 100–123). Lincoln, NE: University of Nebraska Press.

Kapoor, I. (2008). *The postcolonial politics of development*. New York, NY: Routledge.

Kapoor, I. (2012). *Celebrity humanitarianism: The ideology of global charity.* New York, NY: Routledge/Taylor & Francis.

Karabanow, J. (2004). Making organizations work: Exploring characteristics of anti-oppressive organizational structures in street youth shelters. *Journal of Social Work, 4,* 47–60.

Keating, A. (1998). (De)centering the margins? Identity politics and tactical re(naming). In S. K. Stanley (Ed.), *Other sisterhoods: Literary theory and US women of color* (pp. 23–43). Chicago, IL: University of Illinois Press.

Kemmis, S. (2001). Exploring the relevance of critical theory for action research: Emancipatory action research in the footsteps of Jurgen Habermas. In H. Bradbury & P. Reason (Eds.), *Handbook of action research* (pp. 91–102). London, UK: Sage.

Kester, G. (2004). *Conversation pieces: Community + communication in modern art.* Berkley, CA: University of California Press.

Kimpson, S. (2005). Stepping off the road: A narrative (of) inquiry. In L. Brown & S. Strega (Eds.), *Research as resistance: Critical, Indigenous and anti-oppressive approaches* (pp. 73–96). Toronto, ON: Canadian Scholars' Press.

Kincheloe, J. L. (1999). The struggle to define and reinvent whiteness: A pedagogical analysis. *College Literature, 26*(3), 162–194.

Kincheloe, J. L., & Steinberg, S. R. (1998). Addressing the crisis of whiteness: Reconfiguring white identity in a pedagogy of whiteness. In J. L. Kincheloe, S. R. Steinberg, N. M. Rodriguez, & R. E. Chennault (Eds.), *White reign: Deploying whiteness in America* (pp. 3–29). Basingstoke, UK: Macmillan.

Kincheloe, J. L., McLaren, P., & Steinberg, S.R. (2011). Critical pedagogy and qualitative research: Moving to the bricolage. In N. K. Denzin & Y. S. Lincoln (Eds.), *The Sage handbook of qualitative research* (4th ed., pp. 163–178). Thousand Oaks, CA: Sage.

King, T. (2003). *The truth about stories: A Native narrative.* Toronto, ON: House of Anansi Press.

Kivel, D. B., Johnson, C. W., & Scraton, S. (2009). (Re)Theorizing leisure, experience and race. *Journal of Leisure Research, 41*(4), 473–493.

Kleiman, S. (2003). Phenomenology: To wonder and search for meanings. *Nurse Researcher, 11*(4), 7–19.

Kleiman, S. (2004). What is the nature of nurse practitioners' lived experiences interacting with patients? *Journal of the American Academy of Nurse Practitioners, 16*(6), 263–269.

Knights, D., & McCabe, D. (2000). Ain't misbehavin'? Opportunities for resistance under new forms of "quality" management. *Sociology, 34*(3), 421–436.

Knox, S., & Burkard, A. W. (2009). Qualitative research interviews. *Psychotherapy Research, 19*(4–5), 566–575.

Koch, T. (1995). Interpretive approaches in nursing research: The influence of Husserl and Heidegger. *Journal of Advanced Nursing, 21*(5), 827–836.

Kovach, M. (2005). Emerging from the margins: Indigenous methodologies. In L. Brown & S. Strega (Eds.), *Research as resistance: Critical, Indigenous and anti-oppressive approaches* (pp. 19–36). Toronto, ON: Canadian Scholars' Press.

Krafft-Ebing, V. (1877/2006). Psychopathia sexualis with special reference to contrary sexual instinct: A medico-legal study. In S. Stryker & S. Whittle (Eds.), *The transgender studies reader* (pp. 21–27). New York, NY: Routledge.

Kumsa, M. K. (2011). A resettlement story of unsettlement: Transformative practices of taking it personally. In D. Baines (Ed.), *Doing anti-oppressive practice: Building transformative, politicized social work* (2nd ed., pp. 229–248). Halifax, NS: Fernwood Publishing.

Kvale, S. (1996). *InterViews: An introduction to qualitative research interviewing.* Thousand Oaks, CA: Sage.

Ladson-Billings, G. (2000). Racialised discourses and ethnic epistemologies. In N. Denzin & Y. S. Lincoln (Eds.), *The Sage handbook of qualitative research* (2nd ed., pp. 257–277). Thousand Oaks, CA: Sage.

Lane, R. (2008). Truth, lies, and trans science. *Archives of Sexual Behaviour, 37*, 453–456.

Langer, S. J., & Martin, J. I. (2004). How dresses can make you mentally ill: Examining gender identity disorder in children. *Child and Adolescent Social Work Journal, 21*, 5–23.

Langhout, R. D. (2006). Where am I? Locating myself and its implications for collaborative research. *American Journal of Community Psychology, 37*(3–4), 267–274.

Lather, P. (1991). *Getting smart: Feminist research and pedagogy with/in the postmodern.* New York, NY: Routledge.

Lavallée, L. (2009). Practical application of an Indigenous research framework and two qualitative Indigenous research methods: Sharing circles and Anishnaabe symbol-based reflection. *International Journal of Qualitative Methods, 8*(1), 21–40.

Laverty, S. M. (2003). Hermeneutic phenomenology and phenomenology: A comparison of historical and methodological considerations. *International Journal of Qualitative Methods, 2*(3), 21–35.

Lavie, S. (1995). Border poets: Translating by dialogues. In R. Behar & D. A. Gordon (Eds.), *Women writing culture* (pp. 412–427). Berkeley, CA: University of California Press.

Lavie, S. (2011). Mizrachi feminism and the question of Palestine. *Journal of Middle East Women's Studies, 7*(2), 56–88.

Lavie, S. (2012). Writing against identity politics: An essay on gender, race and bureaucratic pain. *American Ethnologist, 39*(4), 779–803.

Lavis, J. N. (2006). Research, public policy making, and knowledge-translation processes: Canadian efforts to build bridges. *Journal of Continuing Education in the Health Professions, 26*, 37–45.

Lawrence, B., & Dua, E. (2005). Decolonizing antiracism, *Social Justice, 32*(4), 120–143.

Leavy, P. (2009). *Method meets art: Arts-based research practice.* New York, NY: Guilford Press.

Lee, B. (2011). Contact and engagement. In *Pragmatics of community organization* (4th ed., pp. 136–149). Toronto, ON: CommonAct Press.

Lemke, T. (2001). The birth of bio-politics: Michel Focault's lecture at the College de France on neo-liberal governmentality. *Economy and Society, 30*(2), 190–207.

Leonard, P. (2003). "Playing" doctors and nurses? Competing discourses of gender, power and identity in the British National Health Service. *Sociological Review, 51*, 218–237.

LeVasseur, J. J. (2003). The problem of bracketing in phenomenology. *Qualitative Health Research, 13*(3), 408–420.

Levin, B. (2008). *Thinking about knowledge mobilization: A discussion paper prepared at the request of the Canadian Council on Learning and the Social Sciences and Humanities Research Council.* Toronto, ON: Canadian Council on Learning.

Levine-Rasky, C. (2013). *Whiteness fractured.* Aldershot, UK: Ashgate.

Linton, S. (1998). *Claiming disability: Knowledge and identity.* New York, NY: New York University Press.

Longman Marcellin, R., Scheim, A., Bauer, G., & Redman, N. (2013). *Experiences of racism among trans people in Ontario.* Retrieved from: http://transpulseproject.ca/wp-content/uploads/2013/03/Racism-E-Bulletin-5-vFinal-English.pdf

Loomba, A. (2005). *Colonialism/postcolonialism: The new critical idiom* (2nd ed.). New York, NY: Routledge.

Lopez, K. A., & Willis, D. G. (2004). Descriptive versus interpretive phenomenology: Their contributions to nursing knowledge. *Qualitative Health Research, 14*(5), 726–735.

Lundy, C. (2004). *Social work and social justice.* Toronto, ON: University of Toronto Press.

Madison, D. (2005). *Critical ethnography: Methods, ethics and performance.* Thousand Oaks, CA: Sage.

Mahoney, J., & Goertz, G. (2006). A tale of two cultures: Contrasting quantitative and qualitative research. *Political Analysis, 14*, 227–249.

Maiter, S., Simich, L., Jacobson, N., & Wise, J. (2008). Reciprocity: An ethic for community-based participatory action research. *Action Research, 6*(3), 305–325.

Marshall, H. L., Craun, S. W., & Theriot, M. T. (2009). The big picture: How social work can effectively utilize photographs. *Social Work, 54*(4), 317–325.

Martinot, S. (2003). *The rule of racialization: Class, identity, governance.* Philadelphia, PA: Temple University Press.

Massaquoi, N. (2011). Crossing boundaries to radicalize social work practice and education. In D. Baines (Ed.), *Doing anti-oppressive practice: Building transformative, politicized social work* (2nd ed., pp. 214–228). Halifax, NS: Fernwood Publishing.

Mayoh, J., & Onwuegbuzie, A. J. (2015). Toward a conceptualization of mixed methods phenomenological research. *Journal of Mixed Methods Research, 9*(1), 91–107.

McDonald, M. G. (2009). Dialogues on whiteness, leisure, and (anti)racism. *Journal of Leisure Research, 41*(1), 5–21.

McEwan, C. (2009). *Postcolonialism and development.* New York, NY: Routledge.

McKenzie, B., & Morrissette, V. (2003). Social work practice with Canadians of Aboriginal background: Guidelines for respectful social work. In A. Al-Krenawi & J. Graham (Eds.), *Multicultural social work in Canada: Working with diverse ethno-racial communities* (pp. 251–282). Toronto, ON: Oxford University Press.

McLean, M. (2003). *The practice of difference in a feminist collective: A critique of transversal politics.* (Unpublished master's thesis.) University of Toronto, Canada.

Meekosha, H. (2011). Decolonizing disability: Thinking and acting globally. *Disability and Society, 26*(6), 667–682.

Meyerowitz, J. (2002). *How sex changed: A history of transsexuality in the United States.* Cambridge, MA: Harvard University Press.

Mirzoeff, N. (1999). *An introduction to visual culture.* New York, NY: Routledge.

Mohanty, C. (2002). "Under Western Eyes" revisited: Feminist solidarity through anticapitalist struggles. *Journal of Women in Culture and Society, 28*(2), 499–535.

Moore, M., Beazley, S., & Maelzer, J. (1998). *Researching disability issues.* Philadelphia, PA: Open University Press.

Moosa-Mitha, M. (2005). Situating anti-oppression theories within critical and difference-centred perspectives. In L. Brown & S. Strega (Eds.), *Research as resistance* (pp. 37–72). Toronto, ON: Canadian Scholars' Press.

Moosa-Mitha, M. (2014). Using citizenship theory to challenge nationalist assumptions in the construction of international social work education. *International Social Work, 57*(3), 201–208.

Moser, C. (2009). Autogynephilia in women. *Journal of Homosexuality, 56*(5), 539–547.

Moser, C. (2010). Blanchard's autogynephilia theory: A critique. *Journal of Homosexuality, 57*(6), 790–809.

Moustakas, C. (1994). *Phenomenological research methods.* Thousand Oaks, CA: Sage.

Mullaly, B. (2002). *Challenging oppression: A critical social work approach.* Don Mills, ON: Oxford University Press.

Namaste, K. (1995). *Access denied: A report on the experiences of transsexuals and transgenderists with health care and social services in Ontario*. Toronto, ON: CLGRO Project Affirmation.

Namaste, V. (2000). *Invisible lives: The erasure of transsexual and transgendered people*. Chicago, IL: University of Chicago Press.

Neuman, W. L. (2006). *Social research methods* (6th ed.). Needham Heights, MA: Allyn & Bacon.

Newberry, A. M. (2012). Social work and hermeneutic phenomenology. *Journal of Applied Hermeneutics*, 1–18.

Nind, M. (2011). Participatory data analysis: A step too far? *Qualitative Research, 11*(4), 349–363.

Nuttbrock, L., Bockting, W., Mason, H., Hwahng, S., Rosenblum, A., Macri, M., & Becker, J. (2011). A further assessment of Blanchard's typology of homosexual versus non-homosexual or autogynephilic gender dysphoria. *Archives of Sexual Behaviour, 40*(2), 247–257.

O'Donoghue, D. (2009). Are we asking the wrong questions in critical arts-based research? *Studies in Art Education, 50*(4), 352–368.

Ohmer, M. L., & Owens, J. (2013). Using photovoice to empower youth and adults to prevent crime. *Journal of Community Practice, 21,* 410–433.

Ollerenshaw, J. A., & Creswell, J. W. (2002). Narrative research: A comparison of two restorying data analysis approaches. *Qualitative Inquiry*, *8*(3), 329–347.

O'Malley, P., Weir, L., & Shearing, C. (1997). Governmentality, criticism, politics. *Economy and Society, 26*(4), 501–517.

Omi, M., & Winant, H. (1986). *Racial formation in the United States: From the 1960s to the 1980s*. New York, NY: Routledge & Kegan Paul.

Ortlipp, M. (2008). Keeping and using reflective journals in the qualitative research process. *The Qualitative Report*, *13*(4), 695–705.

Padgett, D. K. (2008). *Qualitative methods in social work research* (2nd ed.). Thousand Oaks, CA: Sage.

Parada, H., Barnoff, L., Moffatt, K., & Homan, M. S. (2011). *Promoting community change: Making it happen in the real world*. Toronto, ON: Nelson Education.

Pease, B. (2011). *Undoing privilege: Unearned advantage in a divided world.* London, UK: Zed Books.

Penn, G. (2000). Semiotic analysis of still images. In M. W. Bauer & G. Gaskell (Eds.), *Qualitative researching with text, image and sound* (pp. 227–245). Thousand Oaks, CA: Sage.

Pe-Pua, R. (1989). Pagtatanong-tanong: A cross-cultural research method. *International Journal of Intercultural Relations, 13*(2), 147–163.

Perry, P., & Shotwell, A. (2009). Relational understanding and white antiracist praxis. *Sociological Theory, 27,* 33–50.

Phillips, C., & Bellinger, A. (2010). Feeling the cut: Exposing the use of photography in social work education. *Qualitative Social Work, 10*(1), 86–105.

Phipps, D., Johnny, M., & Zanotti, D. (2009). Knowledge mobilization: Turning research into action. *Research Global*, 20–23.

Pickstone-Taylor, S. (2003). Children with gender nonconformity. *Journal of the American Academy of Child and Adolescent Psychiatry*, *42*(3), 266.

Pietersma, H. (2000). *Phenomenological epistemology*. Oxford: Oxford University Press.

Pink, S. (2007). *Doing visual ethnography* (2nd ed.). Los Angeles, CA: Sage.

Plump, B., & Geist-Martin, P. (2013). Collaborative intersectionality: Negotiating identity, liminal spaces, and ethnographic research. *Liminalities: A Journal of Performance Studies, 9*(2), 59–72.

Polkinghorne, D. E. (2005). Language and meaning: Data collection in qualitative research. *Journal of Counseling Psychology*, *52*(2), 137–145.

Pon, G., Gosine, K., & Phillips, D. (2011). Immediate response: Addressing anti-native and anti-black racism in child welfare. *International Journal of Child, Youth and Family Studies, 2,* 385–409.

Potts, K., & Brown, L. (2005). Becoming an anti-oppressive researcher. In L. Brown & S. Strega (Eds.), *Research as resistance: Critical, indigenous, & anti-oppressive approaches* (pp. 255–286). Toronto, ON: Canadian Scholars' Press.

Probyn, E. (1996). *Outside belongings.* New York, NY: Routledge.

Prosser, J. (Ed.). (1998). *Image-based research: A sourcebook for qualitative researchers*. Bristol, PA: Routledge Falmer Press.

Purcell, R. (2007). Images for change: Community development, community arts and photography. *Community Development Journal, 44*(1), 111–122.

Pyne, J. (2014). The governance of gender non-conforming children: A dangerous enclosure. *Annual Review of Critical Psychology*, *11*, 79–96.

Quijano, A. (2000). Coloniality of power and Eurocentrism in Latin America. *International Sociology, 15*(2), 215–232.

Quijano, A. (2008). Coloniality of power, Eurocentrism and Latin America. In M. Morana, E. Dussel, & C. A. Jauregui (Eds.), *Coloniality at large: Latin America and the postcolonial debate* (pp. 181–223). Durham, NC: Duke University Press.

Quinlan, E. (2010). New action research techniques: Using participatory theatre with health care workers. *Action Research, 8*(2), 117–133.

Rainbow Health Ontario. (2013). *Trans health connection*. Retrieved from http://www.rainbowhealthw.penguin.com/trans-health-connection/

Ramirez-Valles, J., Heckathorn, D., V'azquez, R., Diaz, R., & Campbell, R. (2005). From networks to populations: The development and application of respondent-driven sampling among IDUs and Latino gay men. *AIDS and Behavior, 9*(4), 387–402.

Ranger, T. (2001). Colonialism, consciousness and the camera. *Past and Present, 171*, 203–215.

Ranta-Tyrkko, S. (2010). Theatre as social work in Orissa, India: Natya Chetana's theatre for awareness. *Social Work Education, 29*(8), 923–927.

Raymond, J. (1979). *The transsexual empire: The making of the she-male.* Boston, MA: Beacon Press.

Razack, N. (2009). Decolonizing the pedagogy and practice of international work. *International Social Work, 52*(1), 7–19.

Razack, S. H. (2004). *Dark threats & white knights: The Somalia affair, peacekeeping, and the new imperialism.* Toronto, ON: University of Toronto Press.

Reiners, G. (2012). Understanding the differences between Husserl's (descriptive) and Heidegger's (interpretive) phenomenological research. *Journal of Nursing & Care, 1*(5). Retrieved from http://www.omicsgroup.org/journals/understanding-the-differences-husserls-descriptive-and-heideggers-interpretive-phenomenological-research-2167-1168.1000119.php?aid=8614

Reitsma-Street, M., & Brown, L. (2004). Community action research. In W. K. Carroll (Ed.), *Critical strategies for social research* (pp. 303–319). Toronto, ON: Canadian Scholars' Press.

Rejwan, N. (2004). *The last Jews in Baghdad: Remembering a lost homeland.* Austin, TX: University of Texas Press.

Rejwan, N. (2010). *The Jews of Iraq: 3000 Years of History and Culture.* Louisville, KY: Fons Vitae.

Ristock, J. L., & Pennell, J. (1996). *Community research as empowerment.* Don Mills, ON: Oxford University Press.

Robertson, A. (1999). Continuing on the ground: Feminists of colour discuss organizing. In E. Dua & A. Robertson (Eds.), *Scratching the surface: Canadian anti-racist feminist thought* (pp. 309–329). Toronto, ON: Women's Press.

Roger, K. (2000). "Making" white women through the privatization of education on health and well-being in the context of psychotherapy. In A. Calliste & G. Dei (Eds), *Anti-racist feminism: Critical race and gender studies* (pp. 123–142). Halifax: Fernwood Publishing.

Rogers, J. (2012). Anti-oppressive social work research: Reflections on power in the creation of knowledge. *Social Work Education, 31*(7), 866–879.

Rose, G. (2012). *Visual methodologies: An introduction to researching with visual materials* (3rd ed.). Los Angeles, CA: Sage.

Rossiter, A. (2000). The postmodern feminist condition: New condition for social work. In B. Fawcett, B. Featherstone, J. Fook, & A. Rossiter (Eds.), *Practice and research in social work: Postmodern feminist perspectives* (pp. 24–38). New York, NY: Routledge.

Ruch, G. (2005). Relationship-based practice and reflective practice: Holistic approaches to contemporary child care social work. *Child & Family Social Work, 10*(2), 111–123.

Sa'ar, A. (2005). Postcolonial feminism, the politics of identification and the liberal bargain. *Gender and Society, 19*(5), 680–700.

Said, E. (1978). *Orientalism*. New York, NY: Pantheon Books.

Said, E. W. (1993). *Culture and imperialism*. New York, NY: Vintage Books.

Said, E. W. (1997). *Covering Islam: How the media and the experts determine how we see the rest of the world*. New York, NY: Vintage.

Sakamoto, I., & Pitner, R. O. (2005). Use of critical consciousness in anti-oppressive social work practice: Disentangling power dynamics at personal and structural levels. *British Journal of Social Work, 35*(4), 435–452.

Saladaña, J. (2008). Ethnodrama and ethnotheatre. In J. G. Knowles & A. Cole (Eds.), *Handbook of arts in qualitative research* (pp. 195–207). Thousand Oaks, CA: Sage.

Salah, T. (2009). *Writing trans genre: An inquiry into transsexual and transgender rhetorics, affects and politics*. (Unpublished doctoral dissertation). York University, Toronto, Canada.

Sandleowski, M. (2004). Using qualitative research. *Qualitative Health Research, 14*(10), 1366–1386.

San Martin, R. M., & Barnoff, L. (2004). Let them howl: The operations of imperial subjectivity and the politics of race in one feminist organization. *Atlantis: A Women's Studies Journal, 28*, 78–84.

Scheim, A. I., & Bauer, G. R. (2015). Sex and gender diversity among trans persons in Ontario, Canada: A respondent-driven sampling survey. *Journal of Sex Research, 52*(1), 1–14.

Schiele, J. H. (2007). Implications of the equality-of-oppressions paradigm for curriculum content on people of color. *Journal of Social Work Education, 43*(1), 83–108.

Schneider, S. (2013). Producing homeplace: Strategic sites and liminoid spaces for gender-diverse children. In F. Green & M. Friedman (Eds.), *Chasing rainbows: Exploring gender fluid parenting practices* (pp. 111–126). Toronto, ON: Demeter Press.

Schreiber, L. (2000). Overcoming methodological elitism: Afrocentrism as a prototypical paradigm for intercultural research. *International Journal of Intercultural Relations, 24*(5), 651–671.

Schuman, Z. D., Lynch, M., & Abrahm, J. L. (2005). Implementing institutional change: An institutional case study of palliative sedation. *Journal of Palliative Medicine, 8*, 666–676.

Scott, J. W. (1992). Experience. In J. Butler & J. W. Scott (Eds.), *Feminists theorize the political* (pp. 22–40). New York, NY: Routledge.

Scout. (2013, June 13). Déjà vu: National surveys leave trans people behind. *Huffington Post*. Retrieved from www.huffingtonpost.com/scout-phd/national-health-interview-survey-transgender_b_3428446.html

Seawright, G. (2014). Settler traditions of place: Making explicit the epistemological legacy of white supremacy and settler colonialism for place-based education. *American Educational Studies Association, 50*, 554–572.

Sedgwick, E., & Frank, A. (1995). Shame in the cybernetic fold: Reading Silvan Tomkins. *Critical Inquiry, 21*(2), 496–522.

Sengupta, A. (Ed.). (2014). *Mapping South Asia through contemporary theatre: Essays on the theatres of India, Pakistan, Bangladesh, Nepal and Sri Lanka*. New York: Palgrave Macmillan.

Serano, J. (2010). The case against autogynephilia. *International Journal of Transgenderism, 12*(3), 176–187.

Serano, J. (2015). The real autogynephilia deniers. *Whipping Girl Blog*. Retrieved from http://juliaserano.blogspot.ca/2015/07/the-real-autogynephilia-deniers.html

Sewpaul, V. (2006). The global–local dialectic: Challenges for African scholarship and social work in a postcolonial world. *British Journal of Social Work, 36*(3), 419–434.

Sewpaul, V. (2007). Challenging East-West value dichotomies and essentialising discourse on culture and social work. *International Journal of Social Welfare, 16*(4), 398–407.

Seymour, W. S. (2001). In the flesh or on line? Exploring qualitative research methodologies. *Qualitative Research, 1*(2), 147–168.

Sherry, M. (2007). (Post)colonizing disability. *Wagadu, 4*, 10–22.

Shick, C. (2012). White resentment in settler society. *Race, Ethnicity and Education, 1*, 1–15.

Shohat, E. (2003). Reflections of an Arab Jew. Retrieved from http://www.solidarity-us.org/node/626

Shohat, E. (2006). *Taboo memories, diasporic voices*. Durham, NC: Duke University Press.

Shulman, L. (1992). *The skills of helping individuals and groups* (2nd ed.). Itasca, IL: Peacock.

Sin, R., & Yan, M. C. (2003). Margins as centres: A theory of social inclusion in anti-oppressive social work. In W. Shera (Ed.), *Emerging perspectives on anti-oppressive practice* (pp. 25–41). Toronto, ON: Canadian Scholars' Press.

Singer, T. B. (2015). The profusion of things: The "transgender matrix" and demographic imaginaries in US public health. *Transgender Studies Quarterly, 2*(1), 58–76.

Smith, D. (1974). Women's perspective as a radical critique of sociology. *Sociological Inquiry, 44*, 7–13.

Smith, J. M. (2014). Interrogating whiteness within criminology. *Sociology Compass, 8*, 107–118.

Smith, K. (2007). Social work, restructuring and everyday resistance: "Best practices" gone underground. In D. Baines (Ed.), *Doing anti-oppressive practice: Building transformative, politicized social work* (pp. 145–159). Halifax, NS: Fernwood Publishing.

Smith, L. T. (1999). *Decolonizing methodologies: Research and indigenous peoples.* London: Zed Books.

Smith, L. T. (2012). *Decolonizing methodologies: Research and indigenous peoples* (2nd ed.). New York, NY: Zed Books.

Sontag, S. (1982). *A Barthes reader.* New York, NY: Hill and Wang.

Spratt, T. (2005). Radical drama with children: Working with children using critical social work methods. In S. Hick, J. Fook, & R. Pozzuto (Eds.), *Social work: A critical turn* (pp. 105–120). Toronto, ON: Thompson Educational Publishing.

Srivastava, S. (2005). You're calling me a racist? The moral and emotional regulation of anti-racism and feminism. *Signs: Journal of Women and Culture in Society, 31*(1), 29–62.

Srivastava, S., & Francis, M. (2006). The problem of "authentic experience": Story-telling in anti-racist and anti-homophobic education. *Critical Sociology, 32*(2–3), 276–307.

Starks, H., & Trinidad, S. B. (2007). Choose your method: A comparison of phenomenology, discourse analysis, and grounded theory. *Qualitative Health Research, 17*(10), 1372–1380.

St. Denis, V. (2004). Community based participatory research: Aspects of the concept relevant for practice. In W. K. Carroll (Ed.), *Critical strategies for social research* (pp. 292–302). Toronto, ON: Canadian Scholars' Press.

Stone, S. (1996). *The empire strikes back: A posttranssexual manifesto.* In K. Straub & J. Epstein (Eds.), *Body guards: The cultural politics of sexual ambiguity* (pp. 280–304). New York, NY: Routledge.

Strega, S. (2005). The view from the poststructural margins: Epistemology and methodology reconsidered. In L. Brown & S. Strega (Eds.), *Research as resistance: Critical, Indigenous, & anti-oppressive approaches* (pp. 199–236). Toronto, ON: Canadian Scholars' Press.

Strega, S., & Carriere, J. (Eds.). (2009). *Walking this path together: Anti-racist and anti-oppressive child welfare practice.* Halifax, NS: Fernwood Publishing.

Strier, R. (2007). Anti-oppressive research in social work: A preliminary definition. *British Journal of Social Work, 37*(5), 857–871.

Stryker, S. (2006). (De)Subjugated knowledges: An introduction to transgender studies. In S. Stryker & S. Whittle (Eds.), *The transgender studies reader* (pp. 1–17). New York, NY: Routledge.

Tew, J. (2006). Understanding power and powerlessness: Towards a framework for emancipatory practice in social work. *Journal of Social Work, 6*(1), 33–51.

Thobani, S. (2007). *Exalted subjects: Studies in the making of race and nation in Canada.* Toronto, ON: University of Toronto Press.

Todres, L. (2005). Clarifying the life-world: Descriptive phenomenology. In I. Holloway (Ed.), *Qualitative research in health care* (pp. 104–124). London: McGraw-Hill.

Tosh, J. (2011a). "Zuck Off!" A commentary on the protest against Ken Zucker and his "treatment" of childhood gender identity disorder. *Psychology of Women Section Review, 13*(1), 10–16.

Tosh, J. (2011b). Academic debate or transphobic hate? A response to "Zuckergate." *Clinical Psychology Forum, 221*, 51–54.

Tracy, S. J. (2010). Qualitative quality: Eight "big tent" criteria for excellent qualitative research. *Qualitative Inquiry, 16*(10), 837–851.

Travers, R., Bauer, G., Pyne, J., Bradley, K., Gale, L., & Papadimitriou, M. (2012). *Impacts of strong parental support for trans youth: A report prepared for Children's Aid Society of Toronto and Delisle Youth Services*. Trans PULSE. Retrieved from http://transpulseproject.ca/wp-content/uploads/2012/10/Impacts-of-Strong-Parental-Support-for-Trans-Youth-vFINAL.pdf

Travers, R., Pyne, J., Bauer, G., Munro, L., Giambrone, B., Hammond, R., & Scanlon, K. (2013). Community control in CBPR: Challenges experienced and questions raised from the Trans PULSE Project. *Action Research, 11*(4), 403–422.

Trinder, L. (1996). Social work research: The state of the art (or science). *Child & Family Social Work, 4*, 233–242.

Todd, S. (2011). "That power and privilege thing": Securing whiteness in community work. *Journal of Progressive Human Services, 22*, 117–134.

Tower, K. (2000). In our own image: Shaping attitudes about social work through television production. *Journal of Social Work Education, 36*(3), 575–585.

Trachtenberg, A. (1977). *America and Lewis Hine: Photographs 1904–1940*. New York, NY: Aperture.

Tuana, N. (2006). The speculum of ignorance: The women's health movement and epistemologies of ignorance. *Hypatia, 21*(3), 1–19.

Tufford, L., & Newman, P. (2012). Bracketing in qualitative research. *Qualitative Social Work, 11*(1), 80–96.

Turmusani, M. (2003). *Disabled people and economic needs in the developing world: A political perspective from Jordan*. Burlington, VT: Ashgate.

Turner, V. W. (1967). *The forest of symbols*. Ithaca, NY: Cornell University Press.

Twine, F. W., & Gallagher, C. (2007). Introduction: The future of whiteness: A map of the "third wave." *Ethnic and Racial Studies, 1*(31), 4–24.

Usher, P. (1997). Challenging the power of rationality. In G. MacKenzie, J. Powell, & R. Usher (Eds.), *Understanding social research: Perspectives on methodology and practice* (pp. 42–55). London: Falmer Press.

Van Manen, M. (1997). *Researching lived experience: Human science for an action sensitive pedagogy*. London, ON: Althouse Press.

Vazquez, D. (2011). Defining more inclusive social policies for people with disabilities. *Critical Disability Discourse, 3*, 1–13.

Veale, J. (2015). Comments on ethical reporting and interpretations of findings in Hsu, Rosenthal, and Bailey's (2014) "The Psychometric Structure of Items Assessing Autogynephilia." *Archives of Sexual Behaviour, 44*(7), 1743–1746.

Veale, J., Clarke, D. E., & Lomax, T. C. (2008). Sexuality of male to female transsexuals. *Archives of Sexual Behaviour, 37*(4), 586–597.

Wagner, A., & Yee, J. Y. (2011). Anti-oppression in higher education: Implicating neo-liberalism. *Canadian Social Work Review, 28*, 89–105.

Walker, J. A., & Chaplin, S. (1997). *Visual culture: An introduction* (pp. 128–146). New York, NY: Manchester University Press.

Walker, R. (2001). *Black, white and Jewish: Autobiography of a shifting self.* New York, NY: Riverhead Books.

Wallace, R., & Russell, H. (2013). Attachment and shame in gender-nonconforming children and their families: Toward a theoretical framework for evaluating clinical interventions. *International Journal of Transgenderism, 14*(3), 113–126.

Walton, P. (2012). Beyond talk and text: An expressive visual arts method for social work education. *Social Work Education, 31*(6), 724–741.

Ward, J. (2004). "Not all differences are created equal": Multiple jeopardy in a gendered organization. *Gender & Society, 18*, 82–102.

Webb, S. (2001). Some considerations on the validity of evidence-based practice in social work. *British Journal of Social Work, 31*, 57–79.

Weedon, C. (1987). *Feminist practice and poststructuralist theory* (2nd ed.). Oxford: Blackwell.

Wehbi, S. (2010). Critical examination of involvement in social justice efforts: A case example of Canadian international development NGOs. *Journal of Progressive Human Services, 21*(1), 45–65.

Wehbi, S. (2011). Crossing boundaries: Foreign funding and disability rights activism in a context of war. *Disability and Society, 26*(5), 507–520.

Wehbi, S., & El-Lahib, Y. (2007a). The employment situation of people with disabilities in Lebanon: Challenges and opportunities. *Disability and Society, 22*(4), 371–382.

Wehbi, S., & El-Lahib, Y. (2007b). Organizing for the voting rights of people with disabilities in Lebanon: Reflections for activists. *Equal Opportunities International, 26*(5), 449–464.

Wehbi, S., & El-Lahib, Y. (2008). Campaigning for the voting rights of people with disabilities: Case example of the 2005 Lebanese elections. *Disability Studies Quarterly, 28*(2). Retrieved from http://dsq-sds.org/article/view/98/98

Westmarland, N. (2001). The quantitative/qualitative debate and feminist research: A subjective view of objectivity. *Forum: Qualitative Social Research, 2*(1). Retrieved from http://www.qualitative-research.net/index.php/fqs/article/view/974

Westphal, K. R. (2003). *Hegel's epistemology: A philosophical introduction to the "Phenomenology of Spirit."* Indianapolis, IN: Hackett Publishing.

Wiesing, L. (2010). *Artificial presence: Philosophical studies in image theory.* Stanford, CA: Stanford University Press.

Wilson, A., & Beresford, P. (2000). Anti-oppressive practice: Emancipation or appropriation? *British Journal of Social Work, 30*, 553–573.

Wilson, T. J. (1996). Feminism and institutionalized racism: Inclusion and exclusion at an Australian feminist refuge. *Feminist Review, 52*, 1–26.

Wimpenny, P., & Gass, J. (2000). Interviewing in phenomenology and grounded theory: Is there a difference? *Journal of Advanced Nursing, 31*(6), 1485–1492.

Withers, A. J. (2012). *Disability politics and theory.* Halifax, NS: Fernwood Publishing.

Wojnar, D. M., & Swanson, K. M. (2007). Phenomenology: An exploration. *Journal of Holistic Nursing, 25*(3), 172–180.

Yancy, G. (2007). *Whiteness: An introduction.* New York, NY: Routledge.

Yee, J. Y. (2005). Critical anti-racism praxis: The concept of whiteness implicated. In S. Hick, J. Fook, & R. Pozzuto (Eds.), *Social work: A critical turn* (pp. 87–103). Toronto, ON: Thompson Educational Publishing.

Yee, J.Y, & Dumbrill, G. C. (2016). Whiteout: Still looking for race in Canadian social work practice. In A. Al-Krenawi, J. R. Graham, & N. Habibov (Eds.), D*iversity and social work in Canada* (2nd ed., pp. 13–37). Toronto, ON: Oxford University Press.

Yee, J. Y., & Wagner, A. (2013) Is anti-oppression teaching in Canadian schools of social work a form of neo-liberalism? *Social Work Education, 32*, 331–348.

Yee, J. Y., Wong, H., & Janczur, A. (2006). *Examining systemic and individual barriers experienced by visible-minority social workers in mainstream social service agencies: A community project.* Toronto, ON: Access Alliance Multicultural Community Health Centre.

Yee, J. Y., Wong, H., & Schlabitz, T. (2014). Beyond inclusion training: Changing human service and public organizations. In M. Cohen & C. Hyde (Eds.), *Empowering workers and clients for organizational change* (pp. 135–155). Chicago, IL: Lyceum Books.

Yeo, R., & Moore, K. (2003). Including disabled people in poverty reduction work: "Nothing about us, without us." *World Development, 31*(3), 571–590.

Index

156 | Index

policy definition of professional work, 60
positioning
    of activist social workers, 73, 76, 78–
        79, 81–82
    in Advanced Research for Social
        Change course, 113–114, 120–121
    in phenomenology, xii, 89
    as relational, 80–81
    of researcher in disability activism, x,
        23–24
positivism, 4, 5, 117–119
postcolonialism, xi, 43, 44, 46
    See also decolonization
poststructuralism, feminist, 14
Potts, K., 5, 15, 19–20, 27, 96
poverty, 32, 33, 65–66
power
    in knowledge production, 120
    within organizations, 50, 51, 62, 69
    as tenet of anti-oppression research, vii,
        29
    and Trans PULSE, 9
    of white people, 62–63, 67
power relations
    global North/South, x, 18, 20, 26, 43,
        44–46
    need for research to challenge dominant,
        25–26
    participant/researcher, xii, 17, 24–25,
        28, 76, 90, 93, 94, 95, 101
    social worker/service user, 67
    trans people/gender identity clinics, 8
    women of colour/white women, 51
    See also relationships
practice changes and knowledge
    mobilization, 30–31
    See also feminist organization, case
        study on
primary health care workers. *See* activist
    social workers
private vs. public responsibility for social
    welfare, 72
privilege
    academic, 116
    of being ambiguously racialized, 102
    within organizations, 50, 62
    to speak on behalf of the other, ix
    white, 61, 62, 65, 103–104, 116

professionalism, 56–57, 60
programming as barrier to organizational
    change, 57–59
Prosser, J., 42
psychiatric assessment and mental health of
    trans people, 6, 7
psychosocial approach to interviewing, 77

qualitative research
    in analyzing photographs, 43
    applications of, 26–27
    critique of, 68, 82, 84, 93
    in disability studies, 17, 18–19, 20,
        27–28
    identity markers in, 80
    importance of context in, 20–21
    and problems of first-person narratives,
        74–75, 79
    tenets of anti-oppression, 19, 26
    vs. quantitative, 4, 5
quantitative research
    alternatives to, 26–27
    in analyzing photographs, 41–42
    critique of, 4–5
    in Trans PULSE, ix, 3–4, 5–6, 10–12,
        13–14, 15
Quijano, A., 17, 119
Quinlan, E., 36

race
    approach to, xiii
    and photography, 45–46
    researcher's praxis of, 104
    research on, 61, 67–68
    as shifting identity marker, 100–103,
        108–109
racialization
    approach to, xi–xii
    in Canadian institutions, 64
    defined, 63
    of Jewish people, 106–107
    of researcher, 102, 103
    in social service agencies, 61–62, 69, 70
racism
    approach to, xii
    of diversity and multiculturalism, 63
    experienced by researcher, 102, 107
    impact on subjectivities, 82, 83

CPSIA information can be obtained
at www.ICGtesting.com
Printed in the USA
LVHW061043061221
705347LV00011B/3

9 781551 309767